W9-CNV-429

SPEAKING UP

SPEAKING UP

What to Say to Your Boss
and Everyone Else
Who Gets on Your Case

Mark Ruskin

BOB ADAMS, INC.
PUBLISHERS
Holbrook, Massachusetts

Copyright ©1993, Mark Ruskin. All rights reserved. This book, or parts thereof, may not be reproduced in any form without permission from the publisher; exceptions are made for brief excerpts used in published reviews.

Published by Bob Adams, Inc.
260 Center Street
Holbrook, Massachusetts 02343

ISBN: 1-55850-258-0

Printed in the United States of America.

J   I   H   G   F   E   D   C

This book is available at quantity discounts for bulk purchases. For information, call 1-800-872-5627.

This publication is designed to provide accurate and authoritative information with regard to the subject matter covered. It is sold with the understanding that the publisher is not engaged in rendering legal, accounting, or other professional advice. If legal advice or other expert assistance is required, the services of a competent professional person should be sought.
— From a *Declaration of Principles* jointly adopted by a Committee of the American Bar Association and a Committee of Publishers and Associations

COVER DESIGN: Barry Littman

A Note on the Personal Pronoun
To avoid sexism without resorting to such tiresome constructions as *he/she*, *his or hers*, and so on, I have used the masculine and feminine pronouns arbitrarily throughout this book, with about as many *he*s as *she*s.

Visit our home page at http://www.adamsmedia.com

Contents

Introduction

What's the Worst Thing That Can Happen?

Your tongue is practically glued to the roof of your mouth. You're vaguely aware of the taste of pennies. You can't swallow for the fist that's closed around your esophagus. Your heart is beating in your throat and you're sure he can hear it. Your stomach's right behind your heart, rising up into your choking gullet. Your hands are cold, clammy, strengthless. Your knees may snap.

"Well?" he demands. "I'm waiting."

You could be in a blind alley on a rainy midnight, face to face with a man holding a .38 or a switchblade. But the scene is a fluorescent-lit office at ten in the morning, and your boss, unarmed but for his collar pin and power suspenders, is asking why the report due today won't be ready until the end of the week.

You manage to stammer something lame that ends up sounding like you're passing the buck. It only makes things worse. The fact that you sound scared makes your boss think you really screwed up.

Actually, there's a perfectly good explanation for why the report is late. George, in design, didn't have time to get his figures. Mary, in marketing, just finished the demographics Friday. Ellen, in customer service, was so rushed that she sent you the wrong client-response cards. It wasn't just you who didn't have enough time to write the report. *Nobody* had enough time to get you the information *you* needed to write it. The schedule was impossible to begin with, and the only reason you had agreed to it was that you were afraid to tell your boss that you—that everybody—needed more time. So now you're in trouble. You hate being in trouble, but, even worse, you hate yourself for being too scared to explain all this now and, worse still, you hate yourself for having been too scared to speak up in the first place.

To begin with, you might as well stop hating yourself. It won't change anything, and it won't help you the next time. The fact is that your response in this situation was perfectly normal. And it is certainly futile to hate yourself for doing what's normal. "Normal," however, does not necessarily mean "desirable," "useful," "helpful," or—and this is the good part —"inevitable."

Now, at this point, my book could take off in one of two directions. It could take you on a philosophical-inspirational journey, following the path of those who overcame the basic, civilized, human fear of authority, the path of folks ranging from Friedrich Nietzsche to Henry David Thoreau and Mahatma Gandhi, from Martin Luther to Martin Luther King. But let's face it, neither one of us is up to all that just now. You're afraid to speak up to your boss, and I am no philosopher.

So we'll follow another road.

Part One of *Speaking Up* is a how-to-say-it handbook. It makes little attempt to inspire you and no attempt at all to plumb the depths of your soul. What it does provide is a very brief primer on speaking up even when you feel that doing so is absolutely impossible. It outlines strategies for coping with the fear that ties your tongue and keeps you from saying what should or must be said. These are strategies you can use immediately, at the business meeting tomorrow morning or the meeting with your teenager's teacher this afternoon.

This brings us to parts Two and Three. Part Two is devoted to that most intimidating of species, the Boss. The first six chapters explore the beast in all of its varieties, with the emphasis, I regret to say, on the negative—because, after all, the negative is what you are reacting to, and since this book is addressed to you, we'd better begin by dealing with your perceptions and feelings. The next thirteen chapters are devoted to very specific situations with your boss in which you will almost certainly find yourself sooner or later. Each of these chapters begins with a brief how-to section that lays out the essential issues involved in the given situation and then goes on to supply choice words and phrases to use—as well as those to avoid—in handling the situation. But there is more. Rather than philosophize about fear, intimidation, persuasion, and authority, each chapter provides if–then dialogue "scripts" you can actually use in your next encounter.

Who says you can't rehearse your life? Or at least parts of it?

Since bosses are not the only authority figures we face in our world, the nineteen chapters of Part Three deal with a host of other intimidating folk, including your teenager's teacher—in fact, everyone from *A* (Accountant) to *W* (Wine Snob). As in Part Two, each chapter begins with a brief how-to section, followed by words and phrases to use (and not to use) in speaking to the authority figure in question, and conclude with an if–then dialogue script.

How to Use this Book

Speaking Up is a modest book intended to address immediate problems in the real world—*your* real world. If you want to find out, say, how to operate your VCR, you need an owner's manual, not a technical treatise on electronics and television engineering theory. There's nothing wrong with such a book; you just don't happen to need it. Similarly, *Speaking Up* does not take the long way round to get you talking effectively to your boss and anyone else who gets on your case. As you confront each new situation, the only "philosophical" question the book poses—or, rather, asks you to pose—is "What's the worst that can happen?" Answer that question, think it through, run the scenario, and your fear will almost certainly be reduced, perhaps by 10 percent, perhaps by 90 percent. Answer it first, then turn to the words, phrases, scripts, and other practical helps in this book. That's the only philosophy, the only "system" you'll find here, and it is all the instruction you'll need to make this book useful to you.

Part One

A How-To-Say-It Handbook

Feelings, Right and Wrong

The ancient Greeks and the medieval scholars knew the importance of what they called "rhetoric"—the art of persuasive oratory. They studied it, thought about it, and wrote rule books about it, developing and describing formal strategies for persuasion called "tropes." Use this trope to get that result, that one to get this result, and so on. Few of us nowadays are called on to perform as orators, to sway vast populations to our way of thinking. But all of us, every day, need to persuade individuals who loom importantly in our lives. Of course, it is usually somewhat impractical to subject your boss or your physician or the IRS auditor or your landlord to a lengthy, tightly reasoned speech. More often we have only moments to persuade, and those moments are pressured by myriad factors beyond our immediate control, including our emotions and those of our listener. Too often it is during these precious moments, when clarity and strength are most required, that we are assailed by a haze of emotion and intimidating fears that make us go weak in knees and voice. When we most need to, we find that we cannot speak up—or, at least, speak up effectively.

But if feelings interfere with communication, they are also the substance and the object of communication. Where the Greeks and the pundits of the Middle Ages aimed at developing grand systems of rhetoric designed to move the world, most of us today would be satisfied by a kind of micro-rhetoric—a system to aid us in the person-to-person tasks of persuasion that confront us daily. Our micro-rhetoric is designed to accomplish two ends. We want first to be able to speak *through*—or in spite of—whatever negative feelings most often interfere with effective communication. Second, as our rhetoric helps us negotiate a path around our disruptive emotions, it must allow us to create the "right" feelings in others.

Now, as any psychologist will tell you, feelings are neither bad nor good. They just *are*. But as anybody in the business of persuasion—sales, law, advertising, ministry—will tell you, there are "right" feelings and "wrong" feelings. These are not synonymous with moral and immoral. Rather, "right" feelings are the feelings you want your listener to have, the feelings that will make it possible for him to act the way you want him to, while "wrong" feelings are those that motivate him to act contrary to your interests, desires, and needs. I am not suggesting that, when you are trying to persuade someone to your point of view, you abandon all appeal to the rational mind. Certainly it helps motivate action if you can provide intellectually sound reasons to do a certain thing. My point, however, is that in day-to-day, hour-by-hour encounters with others, persuasion is far more often a function of feeling than of full-blown logical discourse. It is usually more efficient and more feasible to pave an emotional road to the actions you wish to motivate—a road along which your listener *chooses* to travel—than it is to lead, push, and cajole your listener in the desired direction by means of logical argument. Browbeat your boss with "good reasons," and eventually you will numb her into ignoring you altogether. Speak to your boss in a way that cultivates the right feelings, and she will be more likely to move in the direction you want her to go.

Manipulative? You bet. And the first person you need to manipulate is yourself. In my introduction I have already suggested an exercise for helping you overcome the crippling feelings that interfere with speaking up: try to imagine the worst thing that can happen to you in the verbal situation you are about to face.

The bad news is that this is about as much as you can do to change how you actually feel, to give *yourself* the right feelings. If, after trying this exercise, you are still uncomfortable—or even terrified—when it comes time to speak up, well, there's nothing either of us can do about it.

The good news is that this doesn't *have* to matter. If you wait for your feelings to change before, say, asking your boss for a raise, you'll probably drift past the age of retirement by the time you're ready to speak up. The great thing about giving people the right feelings is that you don't necessarily have to have the right feelings yourself. All you need are the right *words* uttered in the right way and at an appropriate time.

We are accustomed to thinking that words and acts must have

their origin in feelings. If we don't feel confident, we cannot act boldly. If we don't feel absolutely convinced that we deserve that raise, we can't ask for it effectively. And so on. This interpretation of cause-and-effect is a fiction. Who says that feelings *have* to come before the words? Learn to use the right words first, get what you need, accomplish what you want, and the right feelings will follow.

Beware the Voice of Fear

It would be nice if I could stop right here—just tell you to ignore your fears and move on. Of course, it's not quite that easy. Even if you are able to prepare yourself with the right words, your emotions can choke them back or cause you to deliver them in a voice of fear. You've heard that voice: thin, tight, quavering, high, and utterly unpersuasive—or, rather, tending to move the listener in exactly the opposite direction from the one you want. With each word you utter you realize more powerfully that you are hopelessly scared. Every word becomes more difficult to get out and falls on the ear less persuasively. Soon, you begin to forget all the good words you rehearsed in preparation for this conversation. Then you lose your focus on the ideas you are trying to convey. All you can think about is your fear. You've blown the presentation.

How do you get around the voice of fear? Try thinking of it as just another case of false cause and effect. The great American psychologist William James once declared, "We do not run because we are afraid. We are afraid because we run." This is a tremendously helpful way of looking at things.

Anyone who has been through natural childbirth training—either as a mother or a father or a "birthing partner"—is familiar with the great emphasis placed on breathing exercises and routines. It's important to keep that oxygen flowing to the baby, right?

Well, yes. But, actually, the breathing routines have very little to do with that. Their more central function is to give the mother something to concentrate on. If you are breathing in a regular, self-conscious way—and you're doing it right—you're less apt to scream. If you don't hear yourself screaming, then things can't be all that bad, can they? After all, if you were in real pain and terror, you'd be screaming.

Regular breathing does not radically alter the process of childbirth. But it does focus attention away from pain by, in part, removing one element associated with pain—the scream. Rather than attempt to dislodge the boulder that is your fear, why not simply walk around it? Concentrate not on your fears, but on your voice. Do whatever you can *consciously* and *deliberately* to mold your voice into an instrument capable of a rich, full-bodied sound. Begin by breathing deeply. Take a drink of water for essential lubrication. And deliberately concentrate on pushing your voice down to a lower pitch than what comes naturally. This applies whether you are a man or a woman. A relatively low-pitched voice carries more authority than a relatively high-pitched one. It is also easier to control.

Concentrate on the resonant pitch you have achieved, and slow the pace of your speech to match it. Do what all good singers do: open your mouth when you speak. The volume does not have to be loud—keep it conversational—but force the voice into its lower register, speak more slowly than what comes naturally, and sound out each word deliberately, as if each packet of meaning is valuable to you and your listener. While you are doing all of this, *listen* to yourself. Listen to the resonance of your voice. It's confident, it's convincing, and it's coming from *you*. It should make you feel good.

The voice of fear is almost inevitably paired with the look of fear. The one feeds on the other. We have all heard the expression, to "shrink in fear." Most animals, faced with a danger they can neither fight nor flee, attempt to contract into as compact a physical unit as possible. People do much the same thing. Fearful, we slump, hunch our shoulders forward, cast our eyes downward, and fold our hands down low in front of ourselves. Not only does this broadcast our fear to others, but, as when we hear our own voice of fear, such body language communicates our own fear to ourselves. And, unfortunately, we act accordingly. If I *sound* scared, and I *look* scared, then I must *be* scared.

While you are concentrating on your voice, then, pay heed to your body language. Stand straight; this also makes it easier to speak with full resonance. If you are concentrating on your voice, you will naturally tend to stand quite straight. Make good use of your hands. Gesture with them. Use them to punctuate a point. Do not clasp them in front of you. Do not fold them across your chest; this suggests defensiveness and resistance to whatever the listener may have to say. Do not stand with your hands on your hips; this communicates defiance and impatience. And as your mother undoubtedly told you, don't keep your hands in your pockets. She was right: It makes you look like a little kid.

It is also best to keep your hands away from your face. You should be careful not to cover your mouth when you talk. To begin with, this makes it virtually impossible to understand what you are saying, but, even more important, it suggests shame—that you have something to hide. Rubbing your cheek or forehead telegraphs anxiety, and bringing your hand to the back of your neck communicates your intense desire to leave—to pull yourself out of the situation by the scruff of your own neck.

Your hands are too important to leave to their own devices. Use them as part of your speech. Use them freely in gesture, stopping short of sticking your index finger in the other fellow's solar plexus. You can spread your hands before you, to help you lay out your discourse. You can tick off points finger by finger. You can use your hands to help draw the words out of you. There is nothing wrong with this. It communicates enthusiasm and sincerity while it keeps your hands out of trouble.

Finally, there is one aspect of body language of which everyone is aware: eye contact. We all know how disconcerting it is to talk to someone who persists in looking down or away from us. Unfortunately, it is difficult for most of us to make and hold eye contact, not only for emotional reasons, but simply because most of us have a tendency to look away, to look up and to the side, when we are thinking as we speak. Maintaining eye contact takes deliberate concentration. Before leaving the subject, we should also note that eye-to-eye contact is not, in fact, always the best communication strategy. When you need to underscore your authority, you may find it more effective to fix your glance slightly *above* your listener's eye level, at about the forehead. This tends, mildly, to assert dominance over your listener.

The Matter of Timing

There are two kinds of timing. The first is knowing when and when not to broach a subject. The second is more accurately called pacing, and it makes the difference between a monologue and dialogue.

Many factors determine the best time to bring up a particular subject. Obviously, it's better to ask for a raise after you have successfully completed a project than after you have just been clobbered by a client for screwing one up. The more subtle aspects of timing, however, require you to observe the routine and rhythms peculiar to your office. Generally, Mondays are bad days to raise issues that can be put off until Tuesday. But perhaps you know that Tuesday is the day your boss regularly fights with the comptroller over the reporting of expenses, whereas Thursday is the day that new projects are considered—and that puts your boss in a positive, energetic mood. The objective is a simple one. When you have some control over when a topic is to be brought up for discussion, exploit that element of control deliberately. Don't let over-eagerness propel you into broaching a topic prematurely, and don't allow a penchant for putting things off to cause you to miss a prime opportunity. Become sensitive to the working rhythms of your office, and mesh your important communications with them.

Remember, your day-to-day communications can have consequences (for you, certainly, but perhaps for your company as well) worthy of a major oration. However, your day-to-day communications are not speeches. They are, in essence, conversations. When folks lament the death of the art of conversation, they may think that people have run out of things to talk about. Actually, there's plenty to talk about. What kills conversation is not a dearth of subject matter but a failure of lively interchange, of give and take. You can revive this vital feature of successful conversation by thinking about the pacing of your communications. Do not issue a manifesto, making point after unrelenting point. That's reciting, not talking.

Make a point, then pause, widen your eyes, and lean forward. Invite a response. And, above all, listen to that response. If the pause and look alone are insufficient to elicit a response, you may have to ask for one: "What do you think?" "How does that sound?" Do this sparingly, however; it gets irritating pretty quickly and begins to suggest a lack of confidence—as if you need continual reassurance. Furthermore, be careful to avoid deliberately asking for confirmation: "Am I right?" This forces the listener into a response he may not want to make—or you may not want to hear: *"Sure. Of course. Definitely."* or *"No. You're all wrong."*

Never Beg, Always Bargain

As the rhythm of conversation is give and take, so its spirit is negotiation: asking *and* giving. We do ourselves and our employer a disservice, for example, when we talk about *asking* for a raise. Asking for a raise is not likely to be very successful, and there is no reason why it should be. *Negotiating* for a raise has a far better chance of success. Asking is taking; negotiating is trading one valuable commodity for another. It is taking and giving. Therefore, you can accept it as a reliable maxim that successful communication is almost universally based on negotiation.

Communication based on negotiation is always live, always founded upon and productive of hope.

"Can I have a raise?"

"No."

End of discussion. A dead issue.

"Since I took over the Lummocks account, we've penetrated two major new markets and at least one new territory—and the year's not over yet. Now I'm just starting on the Burdon account. It needs a lot of work, but I feel good about it, and I'm confident that I can do for Burdon what I've done for Lummocks. You've given me a lot of creative freedom, which is great, and I've assembled a terrific team: I'm supervising six people on the Lummocks account, and I'll be putting together eight on the Burdon job, at least at start-up. I've advanced pretty fast here, and I've had to take on a lot of responsibilities. I believe it's time that my salary caught up with my level of achievement and responsibilities."

Plenty of room for discussion here, for negotiation, for give and take: I supplied x services for y salary. I have not only been successful, I've given you more value than you had bargained for. In the years to come, I will give you even more. Therefore, salary y should be increased to z.

This invites a creative response, not automatic negation. It proposes value rendered for value received.

When in Doubt, Learn Something

You would probably not attempt to "wing" a major presentation. Assigned to report on the current market for the latest computer chip, for example, you would at least take the time to gather the relevant facts and figures. You would probably do even more than this in an effort to gauge current trends and predict the future. Is it such a radical notion, then, to prepare for day-to-day conversation?

No law dictates that conversation must be entirely spontaneous. You might try preparing for even the most apparently casual of discussions with your boss or others who make a difference in your life. You need not use all of your research in any given exchange, but it's good to know that it's there. People prepare a lifetime for so-called overnight success. Why not prepare overnight for success the next morning?

Small Talk, Big Results

Not all business communication is focused on specific goals. You don't go into the office to discuss a raise or a major new project every day. But you do *talk* every day.

Contrary to what many old-line managers believe, office small talk is not a waste of time. It is not idle chatter or mere gossip. At least, it need not be. Small talk can raise company morale by forging an office personality and a sense of belonging to a team. Any organization works best when its members are accustomed to seeing one another as fully rounded human beings rather than as the sales manager, or the secretary, or the vice-president. You can influence the quality of office small talk by steering it away from negatives—what is commonly called office gossip—and directing it to subjects of family, background, and outside interests. Take the small talk beyond the office walls. Learn about others, and tell others about yourself.

This is not meant to squelch another important stream of so-called small talk, which is more accurately called shop talk. Much of a company's creative discussion takes place outside of formal meetings and conferences. By all means, do what you can to foster such inventive discussion.

Sticks and Stones

What do you do when disputes arise in the workplace? No job is completely without them. Some disputes are demonstrative, dramatic, and bitter. More often they are quiet. They smolder for perhaps months or even years, giving rise to subtle sabotage and political jockeying that may yield short-term benefits for some individuals but that ultimately reduce the productivity of the company. The best way to handle disputes is to prevent them or, rather, to transform developing arguments into productive discussions. You will find numerous strategies in this book for doing just that. What they all have in common is the goal of focusing discussion on issues rather than personalities. This means that you should attempt to exclude from the discussion words that convey judgment of personality, attitude, or training. "You always take the conservative approach" is almost certain to provoke a fight. Focus instead on the specific issue under discussion: "Let's consider upping that 5,000 to a print run of 8,500." This strategy does not prevent a dispute—nor is it meant to—but it does stop a fight. It is important to your business to argue the merits of a print run of 5,000 versus 8,500. It is at best irrelevant and at worst damaging to your business to spend time arguing about whether so-and-so always takes the conservative approach.

Business is not about avoiding disputes; it is about fashioning disputes that are productive. How do you stand up for yourself? Identify the issues, distinguish these from the personalities involved, and then pit issue against issue rather than ego against ego. If you focus opposing points of view on a particular issue or problem, you don't automatically resolve a dispute, but you do go a long way toward forging disparate personalities into a cooperative team whose members may have differing views but who are nevertheless committed to a common purpose.

Honing Your Verbal Edge: A Few Choice Words

In each chapter of this book you will encounter lists of words and phrases intended to be particularly helpful in a given situation, as well as lists of words and phrases that I suggest you deliberately avoid. These lists are certainly not meant to be exclusive: "Use these words and these words only." Quite the contrary. They are intended as seeds from which you can cultivate your own private garden of language.

How can you hone your verbal edge? By reading dictionaries? By learning a word a day? By using bigger, more impressive words? Unless you happen to be a lexicographer, I don't think any of these is the answer for you. Don't try to learn a bunch of new words. Instead, think about the words you already use. Look at the situations detailed in the various chapters of this book, and examine the lists of words and phrases, as well as the actual scripts, associated with them. How could you, given a similar situation, say what needs to be said better than this book says it? Why is your version better? Now, how could you say it worse? Why is it worse? Imagine the effect of different words on different people in different situations. Would Ms. Slocum prefer to *cooperate* with you in writing the year-end report? Or would she rather *collaborate*? Do you want Bill's *guidance* or his *suggestions* or his *leadership*?

I am a writer of lists. That's how I begin my thinking process about a topic or a problem. You might find it helpful to begin a series of private lists for yourself. Call these lists "A Few Choice Words." Compile them, add to them, winnow them, think about them.

Your emotions—feelings "right" and "wrong"—you will always have. Don't try to ignore them. Don't abandon them, and don't fool yourself into thinking you can do much to change them. They are part of what makes you human, and they are the very fuel that propels you toward whatever personal goals of excellence you set for yourself. But effective communication requires more than the raw fuel of feelings. It requires the shaping of motivation and action, which, in turn, requires the management of feelings.

Manage feelings? It sounds like a heartless undertaking at best and, in any case, an impossible task. So don't try to do it. At least not directly. What you *can* learn to manage are words, the tokens, the products, and the creators of feelings. If what I have to say in this book helps you to think about the language through which we conduct our daily business—both inside and outside of the workplace—I will be satisfied that I have done my job.

Part Two

Your Boss

Type 1: The Tyrant

The tyrant boss thinks he is your parent—not your father or mother, with all the love and concern those roles entail, but your *parent*—authority incarnate, plain and simple, absolute, and not to be questioned. His object is to make you feel like a child in the narrowest and most negative sense: a little person wholly dependent on the parent, incapable of making decisions. The tyrant relies on monologue and avoids dialogue, though he may ask lots of questions. The tyrant is interested in keeping you unstable and unconfident, so that you never quite feel that you are doing an adequate job.

The tyrannical boss likes a big desk, and his chair is always higher than yours. If the boss is a particularly adept tyrant, he will not look you in the eye but in the forehead, as if to press you down with his gaze.

The tyrant boss is not subtle. He thrives on threats. That does not mean that he warns you daily about your performance or that he practices origami with a pink slip while he's talking to you. He does, however, use phrases like, "you'd better," "get a handle on," "get on top of," "get on the ball," and "get on the stick." Clichés are, in fact, very important to the tyrant. In talking to one, you often get the feeling that he is acting out a script.

Well, he *is*. The tyrant has an image of himself, a crude schematic diagram of what a Boss should be, and he acts according to it. He does not see you, and, really, he does not see or hear himself. He is playing a role, and, what is more, he expects you to respond by playing your role. His role is the boss, the man in charge; your role is the worker, the drone, the dependent, the victim.

If, as the saying goes, absolute power corrupts absolutely, how does the relative power your boss commands affect him? All too often, relative power—limited authority—produces the most absolute of tyrants. The manager who occupies a niche midway up the corporate food chain has power to wield and pressure to bear. Just how hard he comes down on you is the product of his power multiplied by the pressure on him. It's a simple equation: If his boss knocks him, he's liable to pound you—and that's why I say that relative authority produces the most absolute tyrants.

Depressing, isn't it? But what happens when you deal not with a middle manager but with, say, the owner, the man who answers to no one? Often this kind of boss is more generous. People who are genuinely in control, who are making their own decisions, tend to apply less pressure to others. Still, it is perfectly possible that you will encounter an owner-tyrant, especially in small firms where money is tight. Such a boss can be an asset one minute and a liability the next.

Now that the bad news is out of the way, the good news is that the tyrant can be dealt with effectively and you need not be at his mercy. Begin by humanizing—or, rather, humbling—your boss. This does not involve anything you say or do *to* him. The humbling takes place in the only arena in which it really matters: your mind. When I was in graduate school, I was greatly intimidated by the chairman of my department. I had trouble talking to him. I even had trouble looking at him. Then, one afternoon, as our class was gathered around the seminar table, I was gazing down at the floor, I suppose to avoid eye contact. It was then that I noticed that Herr Professor was wearing one brown sock and one blue. From that point on, I never had any trouble.

Your boss's socks always match? Find something else to concentrate on. Perhaps he picks his nose when he thinks others aren't looking, or probes his ear? If not, well, just *imagine* him doing this. Perhaps his voice is high. Perhaps his grammar is bad. Or just imagine what he looks like in pajamas. We are all imperfect, and most of us are taught, in charity, to overlook the imperfections in others. Faced with a tyrannical boss, start by ferreting out—in your mind's eye—all the flaws. If you can't find them, make them up. Practice this exercise before you talk to him.

While you are thinking about his foibles, find something to compliment your boss on. Is this sucking up? I prefer to call it "manipulation." Make your boss feel good about something relatively neutral—his choice of necktie, the color of his jacket—while you are imagining how that necktie or that jacket will look when your boss drops his marinara sauce on it. The idea is to put you in control of this encounter. You are used to thinking of yourself as the victim of a tyrant. Now turn the tables by allowing your imagination, your power of fantasy, to tyrannize over your boss. At the same time, remain in conscious control of the situation by deliberately playing the hypocrite. Express your admiration.

Finally, while you are imagining your boss powerless, take steps to empower him in his own eyes. Shift responsibility to him by asking his advice, asking how he might do something. You don't want to make it look as if you can't do your job; rather, that you consider your boss your mentor, someone you admire and from whom you have much to learn. This addresses the tyrant's insecurity in a positive way. Instead of reinforcing his image of the relationship, which is master-slave, victimizer-victim, it creates a more beneficent teacher-student relationship, one that still empowers the boss but in a kinder, gentler way. And, who knows? The worst that can happen is that you'll actually learn something.

Words to Use

advise	margin
better	pleasant
charge	productive
dramatically	profitable
effective	reasonable
effectual	recharge
evaluate	reduce
expedite	revise
experience	smart
great	thanks
helpful	unexpected
improved	valuable
increase	vigorous
intelligent	workable
learn	

Phrases to Use

be grateful for your advice	immediate action
benefit from your experience	immediate response
can you show me	judgment call
how could this have been avoided	like to get your take on this
	plan for the future
how would you go about	realistic reassessment

seek your advice
under control
use your skill

we could not expect
years of experience

Words to Avoid

blind
bungled
cannot
collapse
demand
fault
guess
imagine
insist

loss
lost
mistake
overbearing
overloaded
provoke
stupid
unreasonable

Phrases to Avoid

didn't seem important
dropped the ball
error in judgment
I can't explain
it got by me
it was John's fault
might have
missed the opportunity to
must not

not enough time
should have
talk to John
too much
unreasonable demands
wasn't aware
will not
you don't give me

Your Script

Tyrant: *I'm disappointed in you. I don't like what I see in your sales report for the northwest territory. I want my people selling out there.*

You: *I'm disappointed, too. Sales are not what I had projected. I'm on top of it. I'm calling a meeting of the sales reps. I think it's time we took more control. I was about to come to you to seek your advice on the situation, which I'm sure is something you've handled plenty of times. Of course, I'd also like to get you in on the meeting, and I'd like to talk to you before the meeting so that you can help me clarify the issues and lay out the most effective approach. I want to expedite this. Can I see you at the end of the week and get your take on what I plan to do about the situation?*

The tyrant speaks like a parent ("I'm disappointed in you") and like a tinhorn dictator ("my people"). Cope with the tyrant by quietly refusing to act the part of a child or a peasant. But, while you dodge the personal component of the tyrant's attack, address the substance of

YOUR BOSS • 25

his complaint head on. He's "disappointed"? So are you. Then demonstrate that, while you are taking charge of the situation, you can do so far more effectively with the tyrant's advice and guidance. Don't, however, foist work on the tyrant. He does not want to do your job for you. Assure him that *you* are working: you are eager to present a plan and get his "take" on it. The danger of this scenario is that the opening personal attack will get your defenses up or demoralize you by making you feel like a child. Don't evade criticism, but do get out from under your tyrant boss's parent-child fantasy. Find a way to empower your boss without relinquishing your own strength.

Responses to Anticipate

Are you asking me to do your job for you?
Reply with:

☑ *No, I am not. But I am asking for your advice so that I can do my job more effectively.*

This talk is all fine, but I'm just not sure you are motivated.
Reply with:

☑ *You don't have to worry about that. I am motivated. I like to win, and I like to be on a winning team. That's why I want to take advantage of your experience.*

Do you think you can get your people out there selling?
Reply with:

☑ *I know I can—especially with your help. We'll turn this around.*

Type 2: The Guiltmonger

My first boss was a failed guiltmonger. He was the manager of a drugstore I worked in one summer between junior and senior year in high school. He was a small man who sweated profusely and was afflicted with a peculiar tic that convulsed his entire forehead in a kind of squint that started up above his eyebrows. He was frantic much of the time and overworked all of the time. This was because he never successfully delegated a task. He would show me how he wanted something done, and in the process he would do the job himself. His efforts were sometimes punctuated with phrases like, "This is asking too much of you" or "I'd better do this part myself," or "You're probably not ready for this yet."

Most of my summer's employment was spent standing next to him watching him do my job. It wasn't fun, and it certainly did not make me feel good. In fact, he could have had me do almost anything—I felt so guilty. Here was this poor little fellow working himself to death, all on my account. He was a natural guiltmonger. Unfortunately for him, he didn't realize his talent and never capitalized on it. He really did do all the work—of all his employees—and, as a consequence, his store was understocked, poorly maintained, and rarely patronized. The difference between him and the legion of successful guiltmongers is that they carry the relationship through to its logical conclusion. They get *you* to do the work—and not just your work, but the work of two or three others, with late hours and weekends thrown in for good measure.

The successful guiltmonger is the mirror image of the tyrant boss. She does not attempt to tower over you; instead, she shows you how you are tearing *her* down by your unwillingness to make "that extra effort." She will not threaten to fire you, but she will suggest that, unless "that extra effort" is made, the business will dissolve and you and everyone else will be out of work. She will not tell you or even ask you to put in overtime, but will look up from her desk at 5:30 and say something like, "Oh, no, don't stay late. You have more important things to do, like have dinner with your family. My family has gotten used to my working late by now." She's fond of phrases like, "Somebody's got to do it—but don't you worry about it." "I don't know where we're going to find the bodies to do this job," she may say, "but we'll have to manage—somehow." The guiltmongering boss teaches you the true meaning of the term *passive aggressive* with such favorite lines as,

Don't trouble yourself.
Think nothing of it.
No—really—we'll manage without you.
I understand what it means to have a family.
Oh, you have a life *outside of the office?*
I don't remember what my husband looks like.
I can't remember the last time I had dinner at home on a weekday.
We'll find somebody to do it.
If you can't do it, you can't do it.
If you're not available, you're not available.
I can't expect you to do that.
I guess we'll manage.
Listen, you don't owe me any overtime.

The tyrant boss causes great anxiety, but if you successfully cope with him on a given occasion, you come away from the encounter feeling pretty good. You never come away from a transaction with the guiltmonger feeling good. There are only degrees of bad feelings, and the best you can hope for is coming away from the encounter without feeling too guilty and, above all, without having been manipulated.

Your guiding strategy in dealing with the guiltmonger is always to separate your commitment to your job, the company, and your career from your relationship to your boss. Depending on how you feel about your work and what you realistically need to accomplish in order to do your job, you may have little choice about putting in overtime or pushing extra hard to meet a deadline. The crucial step is separating the unavoidable demands that come with the territory from the emotional demands that come from a manipulative guiltmonger. The fact that your boss makes you feel guilty does not absolve you from doing your job responsibly.

Once you have successfully distinguished between emotion and necessity, you need to help your boss do the same. There are two ways to accomplish this. If an unreasonable demand is made on your time and you have a legitimate excuse, use it. "Normally, I could work overtime, but today's our anniversary," or "I wish I could change my day off, but I have a medical appointment that would take months to reschedule," and so on. The problem with relying on such excuses is that, since the guiltmongering boss is by definition chronic with her demands, you will soon run out of legitimate excuses and you will be perceived as uncooperative. The second response to the guiltmonger, then, is to administer a calm dose of reality. "Well," your boss says, "I suppose I'll just stay here and work on this report myself." You reply, "Do you think that's necessary? You know, I'll be all yours tomorrow from eleven till three. I could rough out a draft, and you could review it." Or, "Do you think it's a good idea to do something this important in such a hurry? Why don't we review it together first thing in the morning?" Avoid making the exchange a contest of passive-aggressive persuasion by pointing out, in a positive but nonemotional way, the alternatives to either of you making an undue sacrifice. Yes, you assure your boss, you will do the necessary work, but at a time and in a manner that will be convenient for everyone and that is most likely to result in a job well done.

Words to Use

acceptable
accomplish
adequate
careful
cooperate
efficient
feasible
mistake
necessity
oblige
plan
priority

prudent
reasonable
rush
schedule
time
together
unavoidable
urgent
we
willing
workable

Phrases to Use

clear the decks
first thing in the morning
go over this with you
Haste makes waste (yes,
    you really can say this)
high priority
I can give you [amount] of
    time this week
I can give you all the time
    you want on [day]

I'll help you out until [time]
    and then all day
    tomorrow
more effective
most effective use of
    resources
plan this out
proceed methodically
review this in the morning
schedule this
we can do it together

Words to Avoid

cannot
deadline
delay
later
no

ultimatum
unfair
unreasonable
won't

Phrases to Avoid

bail you out
can't do it
demanding too much
glad you can handle it
    yourself
good luck
if you are really in a jam

I hate to see you work so
    hard
I have other things to do
I'm overloaded
in a few days
I really don't want to do this
I really wish I could help

*it's a shame you have to
    work so hard*
I won't
then do it yourself
*then you don't need me to
    do it*
*then you don't need me to
    stay*

this is unfair
this screws up all my plans
too busy
too much work
unable to do it
very soon now
you owe me one

Your Script

Guiltmonger: *I suppose we can manage—somehow—if we don't get this report in tomorrow. I'll make some excuse or other.*

You: *I agree. It seems to me a lot better to take the time to do this thing right than to try to rush it through tonight. I can give you all day tomorrow. I'll rough out a draft, and we can go over it together—dot all the i's and cross all the t's—and then we'll have something we don't have to bite our nails about. You don't have to make any excuses. We need time to do a good job.*

The guiltmonger works from emotion and expects you to respond emotionally. Don't. Instead, respond to the overt content of the guilt monger's statement, not the passive-aggressive meaning you are meant to read between the lines. By "suppose we can manage," the guiltmonger really means, of course, "I'll look bad if you don't do tomorrow's work today." Instead of picking up on this childish crypto-meaning, respond positively to the suggestion that we can, indeed, manage. Build on it. Yes, not only can we manage, but, if we take our time and do a good job, we can manage more successfully.

Responses to Anticipate

Well, I guess I'll just sit down and do what I can myself.
Reply with:

☑ *Why do that when I can give you all the help you want tomorrow? You deserve the night off.*

It makes me nervous to work so close to a deadline.
Reply with:

☑ *That's why we need to approach this methodically and at a time when I can give you a hundred percent. We'll sort it out together and get it in on time.*

I guess it is unfair to ask you to do so much extra work.
Reply with:

☑ *It's not a question of fairness, but of making the most productive use of my time.*

It would help if you could reschedule your appointment this evening.
Reply with:

☑ *I wish I could, but it's impossible on such short notice.*

Type 3: The Blamer

One of the most successful shows ever to air on television was "The Fugitive," in which one Richard Kimball, unjustly convicted of murdering his wife and under sentence of death, escapes to pursue the real killer while evading the police lieutenant obsessed with recapturing him. What was the show's formula for success? In two words: audience identification. Most of us respond powerfully to the nightmare situation of an innocent person accused of wrongdoing because most of us have been in similar (if far less dire) situations—or at least fear that we will be blamed unjustly for something sooner or later. Most likely the fear taps into our experience of childhood, those supposedly carefree days when parents and teachers liberally issue blame without bothering much about assessing guilt or innocence.

Like parents, bosses can also be prodigal with blame. Sometimes this is a conscious attempt to dodge responsibility. Sometimes it is an unconscious response to a situation gone sour. Sometimes it is direct and cutting.

Before we discuss strategies for verbally coping with the blamer, we need to make some distinctions. First, it is necessary to distinguish between those times when you are at fault and those times when you are not. If you have made a mistake, own up to it, confront it, deal with it, and repair it. Second, distinguish between the boss who, on rare occasions, wrongly assigns blame and the habitual blamer, for whom blaming is an integral part of management style.

We will deal with handling your bona-fide screw-ups in "Situation 10: Accidents and Errors," so let us turn first to confronting the occasional accusation from an otherwise substantially stable boss. Begin by getting the facts. Do not deny anything before you have the full story; that will just make you seem defensive. Collecting the facts will accomplish two things. First, it will calm your boss down by shifting his focus from personalities to events. Second, it will give you the opportunity not only to demonstrate your blamelessness, but, quite possibly, lead to the resolution of the problem in question.

If you must deal with a habitual blamer, begin the same way. Focus calmly on the facts. Confront the events rather than the accusation. Getting to the facts is not easy when you are dealing with a habitual blamer. The blamer's object is to shift responsibility from himself to you. The last thing he is interested in is facts that may hinder him in this endeavor. The only thing you can offer to counter this is a willingness to accept responsibility, not blame. That is, you need to communicate that, while a given snafu is not your *fault*, you are prepared to accept it as your *problem* and work to resolve it. The blamer-boss may resent your challenging him, but he will not turn down your offer to take on the task of correcting a problem. In this case, your boss has not succeeded in defeating you by wrongly fixing blame on you; you have prevented that. But, at the same time, by offering to help resolve the problem, you have allowed him to feel *as if* he has won.

Manipulative? You bet.

But it is for your own good and, not incidentally, the good of your company.

Words to Use

alternative	*opportunity*
analyze	*positive*
assess	*priority*
best	*rational*
business	*reason*
circumstances	*recover*
consider	*remedy*
discover	*repair*
discuss	*revamp*
effectively	*revise*
efficiently	*rework*
facts	*solution*
fix	*solve*
inventive	*talk*
logical	*try*
new	*volunteer*

Phrases to Use

back on track
best effort
capitalize on
damage control
effective solution
figure out
find a way
get behind and push

get to the bottom of
give you a hundred percent
make the best of
move quickly
positive action
put our heads together
work it out together

Words to Avoid

airhead
blame
bonehead
catastrophe
cornered
delinquent
#%&$@@!*
disaster
dolt
fault
hopeless

idiot
loser
lunch meat
meathead
moron
negligent
numbskull
relax
stupid
tired
witless

Phrases to Avoid

as usual
backed into a corner
bail out
calm down
chill out
he always does that
I wasn't even here
it's her fault
it's not my fault

it's not my job
it's not my responsibility
left hanging
lighten up
out to lunch
so what else is new
twisting slowly in the wind
you always do that

Your Script

Blamer: *Well, you've really done it this time. I turn my back for five minutes and everything goes to hell. The warehouse says it has no record of any of these orders. How do you think we make money? We take orders, transmit orders, and ship orders. How could you have screwed up so badly?*

You: *Mr. Bickler, this is the first I've heard of a problem. Please give me the details so that we can get to the bottom of it and arrive at a solution quickly.*

Blamer: *This is the first you've heard about it? Where have you been?*

You: *I've been right here, but you've been stuck with fielding this complaint. Suppose you let me in on the details so that I can help get us back on track. What I need to get started is the whole story. Then I will do whatever is necessary to fix the problem.*

Blamer: *I don't know that you can "fix" anything.*

You: *Mr. Bickler, I certainly cannot if I don't know what went wrong. Let's go over this situation together.*

The blamer does not see you. He sees only a target. Begin bringing him back to reality by deliberately using his name. Keep the exchange on a human level. At the same time, you must work very diligently and with great control to avoid responding to a personal attack. At all costs, try to focus the exchange on the circumstances and facts of the situation in question. Do not accept or reject blame until you have the whole story, but from the beginning, volunteer to find a solution.

Responses to Anticipate

Don't try to wiggle out of this.
Reply with:

☑ *That's the last thing I want to do. What I want is to get into this problem and start fixing it.*

You have to take responsibility for this.
Reply with:

☑ *That is exactly what I want to do. Let me work with you to fix the problem. Let's begin by going over the facts, so that we can agree on a solution.*

You better do it yourself and do it right now.
Reply with:

☑ *I'll give it top priority. It will save us both time if we begin by going over the facts now.*

I'm too angry to go into details now.
Reply with:

☑ *I'll do what I can now. But I'm going to have to discuss this with you later. I'll give you a buzz in about an hour.*

Type 4: The Dreamer

There is a powerful myth that great ideas and inventions are born from slight sparks of inspiration. An apple dropped on Isaac Newton's head, and he formulated the theory of gravity. Beethoven heard a knock at his door—tap, tap, tap, taaap—and wrote the *Fifth Symphony*. Samuel F. B. Morse had a casual conversation with a scientist on an oceanliner and invented the telegraph. And so on. Why is this myth so appealing? Maybe because it is often true. Great projects *have* been born in fleeting impressions and momentary thoughts. And if it has happened to others, why not to ourselves? All that's needed is a certain spark . . .

Well, that's not quite all. You need that spark, all right, but it also helps to be a genius—a Newton, a Beethoven, a Morse. This requisite has not stopped a legion of bosses from believing that their every passing idea bears the seeds of greatness. These are the dreamers. Dreamers call you into the office and say something like, "While I was driving in this morning I hit a pothole. I thought, 'Why can't R & D come up with a sensor that will alert the driver to a pothole in time to avoid it?' We've got the technology, and we've got the marketing muscle. I want you to start working on this right away."

Suddenly you are swept away in your boss's stream of consciousness, the victim of an idea that happened to drift by.

My object here is not to tell you how to dodge every idea your boss comes up with. After all, it *is* possible that she might come up with something good, profitable, even brilliant. Moreover, I cannot tell you how to distinguish a good idea from an unworkable one. There are no general rules for determining this in all fields. Finally, you may have no choice but to act on whatever assignment your boss hands out. Depending on your position and the way in which your company is organized, it may not even be appropriate for you to render an opinion. What I *can* suggest are some verbal strategies to use in responding to the dreamer without getting sidetracked or derailed.

In movies of a certain period, when someone drifted off into a hallucination, a sharp slap across the face was sufficient to bring him back to reality. This option is generally not available to you. Nor is it a good idea to respond with the verbal equivalent of a slap: "That's crazy!" "It'll never work." "We can't do that." "If I stayed up all night I couldn't come up with a worse idea." You should even avoid such mild but still preemptive remarks as, "I'm not sure this will work," "I'm not sure this will fly," "I don't know that this is feasible," and so on. Unless your opinion is directly solicited—or unless you really do think the idea is a good one—it is usually best to withhold judgment and respond instead to the mechanics of your boss's request or direction. "What kind of priority do you want me to give this?" Or, "Should I put the Balderdash account on the back burner?" In short, respond on the positive side of absolute neutrality, but respond in a way that tends to return your boss's focus to day-to-day reality. If I pursue your whim, your message says, then this, that, and the other will have to be rescheduled, delayed, or sacrificed.

Never say directly that you don't have time to act on the dreamer's idea. That dismisses both the idea and the person behind it. Instead, allude to the context in which work on the idea will have to exist. This will accomplish two things: It will put the idea in perspective, perhaps taking some of the wind out of the dreamer's sails and some of the pressure off you. And it will also convey the message that you are taking the idea seriously enough to make it a part of the company's daily activities. You are already concerning yourself with scheduling action on it.

Beyond the initial dose of reality, fully exploit whatever procedures your company has in place for dealing with new ideas, concepts, and programs. If you must fill out forms or write up a report, get your boss involved in this. "Okay. The first step will be a preliminary P and L. I'll get the paperwork started and bring it in tomorrow." Remember, the object is not to avoid work but to avoid as much unnecessary and wasteful work as possible. It is also to head off the development of an unworkable idea that may soon become your responsibility and, ultimately, your failure. Yet you must accomplish this without alienating your boss. With this in mind, you might reply to the dreamer with, "This is very interesting. Give me some time to think about this. I imagine I'll have lots of questions for you." Take up the task, but don't hop on the bandwagon.

Words to Use

analyze	potential
build	priority
fast track	questions
interesting	resources
intriguing	schedule
investigate	study
management	think
possibility	

Phrases to Use

assess the potential
best management of
    resources
build on this
do some research
examine the possibilities
exciting possibilities
get moving on this

get the ball rolling
interesting potential
profit and loss
resource management
slot it in
will have questions for you
will prepare a list of
    questions for you

Words to Avoid

can't
genius
immediately
impractical
no

right away
surefire
today
unfeasible

Phrases to Avoid

absolutely no time
been done before
can't miss
devote full time to
get to it when I can
I don't have time right now

I don't think so
I'm not sure
love it
sure thing
too much on my plate
won't work

Your Script

Dreamer: *I was watching television last night, and I got an idea. We should do our Annual Report as a music video. I mean it. Set those dry facts to music. It would get us publicity and stir up the investors. I want you to get this started.*

You: *I've got the Philbin project in final phase, and I'm pitching the Ravenswood account. Do you want me to turn these over to someone else to clear the decks for the video? We're talking about a good deal of business there.*

Dreamer: *No. You'd better see those through.*

You: *Okay. Then I'll schedule the video project after those. Let me think about it a bit and rough out a list of questions and issues for you before we move ahead.*

Avoid addressing the merits (or idiocy) of the proposed project. Address instead its impact on present reality. Don't rudely shake your boss into the waking world, but make it possible for her to take herself down from the clouds.

Responses to Anticipate

I want you to give it your full attention.
Reply with:

☑ *Okay. But I'd better begin by giving you a report on my current projects, so that we can reschedule and reassign.*

I don't want this to disappear into limbo. I want to see follow-through.
Reply with:

☑ *Give me some time to review the idea, and I'll prepare a list of questions and issues for you. I also need to discuss my current assignments, so that we can reschedule. I'm pretty heavily committed.*

What do you think about this?
Reply with:

☑ *Sounds like it's worth thinking about. Let me give it some consideration and discuss it with you.*

This is something we really need to be doing, and we need to move fast.
Reply with:

☑ *I'll start sketching out some ideas of the kind of resource commitment the project's likely to involve, and I'll get back to you with any questions.*

Type 5: The Bumbler

To the outsider looking in, the bumbling boss can seem an endearing character—always forgetting appointments, neglecting details, habitually waffling when decisions are called for, stumbling over names, places, money owed, and money due. But to those who work for him, the bumbler is about as lovable as Captain Queeg. The Tyrant may cause more anxiety, the Guiltmonger more grief, the Blamer more resentment, and the Dreamer more pointless work, but for inducing a state of chronic panic, no one can top the Bumbler. He is the captain of your ship. The waters abound in reefs and breed sharks. Good luck.

It is in your best interest to develop verbal strategies that will help the bumbler. You must resist the repeated temptation to express your impatience or even to make fun of him. You will often need to confirm instructions and to correct errors, but you must do this without the least trace of mockery or a patronizing tone. Dealing effectively with the bumbler is an exercise in role playing. One minute you are the employee and your boss is the boss; the next minute you are the teacher and your boss is a somewhat backward student. It is a difficult balancing act that takes considerable sensitivity to pull off successfully.

Words to Use

careful

checklist

concept

confirm

describe

double check

example

model

outline

punch list

repeat

rundown

understand

Phrases to Use

confirm my understanding

confirm the priority

go over

help me to understand

make certain I've got it right

make sure I'm doing what you want

proceed carefully

same wavelength

Words to Avoid

excuse

inept

lunkhead

mistake

slow

sorry

stupid

Phrases to Avoid

I'll tell you again

is that clear

I told you already

now let's see if we can do this right

over and over again

this time

your error

Your Script

Bumbler: *Did you ever send that report to what's-his-name?*

You: *Let me make sure I know which report you mean. To Smith or to Perkins?*

Bumbler: *Smith, of course.*

You: *That report was to be ready by the end of the week. Do you*

YOUR BOSS • 39

need it sooner?

Bumbler: *It should never have been delayed until the end of the week.*

You: *I can revise some things and get it out sooner. I'll shuffle my schedule and prepare the Smith report for Wednesday. Does that sound workable to you?*

The bumbler invites correction. Resist the invitation. Focus instead on clarifying and confirming instructions.

Responses to Anticipate

I'm really getting forgetful.
Reply with:

☑ *No harm done. Let me just run down the list again to make sure we're on the same wavelength.*

I don't see how I can make myself any clearer.
Reply with:

☑ *It was a misunderstanding. We're in synch now. Let me just confirm some things.*

Are you calling me stupid?
Reply with:

☑ *Of course not. I just want to make absolutely certain that I understand what you want before I get started again.*

Am I forgetting something?
Reply with:

☑ *Let's review what you want.*

Type 6: The Emotional Volcano

You learn to look for the Early Warning Signs: a pulsating vein in the forehead, a narrowing of the eyes, a twitch of the cheek in the manner of Bogart or Eastwood. Perhaps you can get away in time. There's a chance of that. But what's inevitable is the explosion itself—an eruption of emotion and invective sometimes accompanied by ranting, finger jabbing, and fist pounding. Then, as the volcanic activity subsides, a period of internal upheaval often follows, a seething of dark feelings directed against you. The message is that you've wounded your boss. You've disappointed her. It is a black, black day.

The emotional volcano is, by definition, a poor manager. True, fear of the boss is a great motivator. It motivates passivity, the stifling of imagination, and the avoidance of confrontation with the boss—which means the avoidance of communication. Most of all, it motivates the employee to seek alternative employment. But if you are stuck in a situation with an emotional volcano, you do have a variety of verbal options for dealing with him or her. Begin first by understanding the basis of your boss's tendency to act on her feelings, and then think through your own response to those feelings.

As a child, I was afraid of bees. I had gotten stung once or twice, and it hurt. My mother tried to get me to overcome my fear by telling me that the bee was more afraid of me than I was afraid of it. I have to admit, that didn't help a bit, but I'm going to tell you the very same thing about your boss anyway. Few things produce such strong emotions as fear, and the engine that drives the emotional volcano is nothing more or less than fear.

What does your boss have to be afraid of? Plenty. If she has bosses to answer to, she suffers the same anxieties and pressures you do. If she owns the company, the consequences of failure, the sense that work is slipping, that profits are dwindling, that the business is leaking, triggers terrible emotions. Running a business is a complex proposition dedicated to a terrifyingly simple goal: survival. In the anxiety-afflicted, insecure boss, the slightest reverse—a late report, a lost sale—seems like the first step down the slippery slope not to a bad day, a poor month, or even a weak quarter, but to death itself.

When one Neanderthal confronted another over a single saber-toothed tiger steak, one of two things happened. The less imaginative Neanderthals beat each other with clubs until only one was left to consume the steak. The more imaginative shared the steak and worked together to hunt up more afterward. The emotional volcano is the less imaginative Neanderthal.

That leaves you to choose the way of the club or the way of the imagination. The eruption of the emotional volcano produces two kinds of fear. One is the simple fear of losing your job—the thought that, in her rage, your boss will summarily fire you. Is this realistic? The fear is certainly real, and losing your job can be a terrible thing, especially if you live from paycheck to paycheck. There is no denying, either, that people do get fired. But it is seldom an act of anger, and most employees are let go because of relatively long-term economic reasons, not the immediate result of an emotional exchange.

You may still think that your primary fear is of losing your job. In fact, what you fear more is actual violence. You may know in your head that the one thing your boss will not do is strike you and the one thing you will not do is lash out at her. But at some level of consciousness you imagine an exchange between Neanderthals. Verbal violence is always a symbol of physical threat. Your boss represents power and authority. In a heated exchange, your imagination gives concrete shape to those abstractions. Your boss, you feel, has the power and authority to crush you. Equally anxiety provoking is the feeling you may have of wanting to fight back, to crush her before she gets you. Of course, you *know* that none of this will happen. But you *feel* it nonetheless.

Fear is a primitive emotion. You can neither avoid nor escape it, but you don't have to be governed by it. Once the volcano erupts, it is best to let the lava flow around you. Force yourself to listen to the tirade, while standing, if possible, with your arms at your sides. Force yourself to look into your boss's eyes, as if you were having a regular conversation. At some natural pause—a lull in the storm—inject calm. This does not mean that you tell your boss to calm down. Never *tell* an angry person to do anything. It will only make her angrier. Nor should you tell her how to feel ("There's no reason for you to be so upset"), since meddling with another's emotions is also likely to elicit nothing but additional rage. Instead, acknowledge the other person's anger: "I can see that you are mad as hell, and I can't blame you, but . . . " The *but* is the point at which you introduce alternatives to the tirade: " . . . but I need to talk this through with you. Would it be better for me to come back and discuss this, or do you want to sit down and go over it now?"

Think back to the last time you were really angry. I had words with an acquaintance once, not very nice words. But none of the words really got to me until he called me *rude*. I don't know why that silly word set me off, but it did. (Norman Mailer says somewhere that you can accuse a man of the most heinous of crimes, and it won't bother him half as much as accusing him of bad manners.) We didn't come to blows, but I did see red—quite literally. My vision narrowed momentarily to a kind of red tunnel. That is what anger does. It imposes a narrow tunnel vision, which prevents consideration of alternatives. Your task in confronting the emotional volcano is to make the alternatives visible: We can discuss this. We can resolve this. We can sit down together. We can do it now. Or we can do it later.

Give your boss some choices, some alternatives. Compel her, in this way, to *think* for a moment rather than *feel*. As for yourself, while you should not meekly submit to abuse, neither should you yield to the temptation to jump into the shouting match. Once the two of you are yelling, the anger is in charge. You won't win the fight and neither will your boss. A third party—rage—triumphs. Listen unmoved. Then provide some choices and alternatives.

This strategy may work, but it is not foolproof. What happens when the tirade continues or even intensifies? The most effective move you can make is out. Separate yourself from your boss. This does not mean that you storm out of the office. Excuse yourself: "Excuse me, Ms. Vesuvia. I can appreciate how angry you are, and, because of that, I think it would be best if I went down to my office for a while. Why don't you buzz me downstairs when we can sit down and talk about this problem without yelling at one another."

Don't tell her that you can't stand her outrageous behavior, but imply instead that neither of you is in a condition to talk productively just now. In this way, you stand a better chance of breaking the circuit of anger without provoking more by indignantly walking out or by staying until you, too, boil over.

Words to Use

alternative	*improve*
appreciate	*negotiate*
aware	*reason*
better	*recognize*
choice	*review*
choices	*revise*
choose	*settle*
elaborate	*strategy*
expedite	*study*
explain	*talk*
formulate	*understand*
illustrate	*withdraw*

Phrases to Use

come back later	*step back and study*
explain what you would like me to do	*take time out*
reason this out	*think this through*
sit down and talk	*work it out*

Words to Avoid

calm	*mean*
excuse	*nasty*
fault	*no*
insult	*relax*
loud	

Phrases to Avoid

calm down	*settle down*
I won't	*what did I do?*
I won't stand for that	*you can't talk to me like that*
keep your shirt on	*you don't know what you're*
nobody says that to me	*talking about*
prove it	

Your Script

Volcano: *I'm tired of things going wrong around here. I'm tired of nothing getting followed up on. You and your department better shape up, because I'm getting tired of all of you. This is a tough, push, push, push business. And if you stop pushing, you just don't survive. Well, let me tell you something right now. You're going down before I do, and that's a promise. I'm tired of being jerked around like this.*

You: *I see that you're damn angry about sales this quarter. So am I, but this is something we need to talk through. We can sit down now over this, or, if you like, I'll come back at a better time, when we can hammer out a strategy. It's up to you.*

Do whatever is verbally necessary to transform the dynamic from *me* against *you* to *us* against the *problem*. Subtly suggest postponing discussion until emotions have cooled.

Responses to Anticipate

I don't want to waste my time talking to you.
Reply with:

☑ *Then I'll go back down to my office. You can give me a buzz if you do decide to discuss this further.*

I'm not finished with you yet.
Reply with:

☑ *I'm sure there's a lot more to say. I'd prefer to come back at a better time, but I'm willing to continue talking if we can conduct this as a conversation and not as a shouting match.*

We have to hash all of this out right now.
Reply with:

☑ *Then I suggest that we sit down, calmly lay out the issues, and act on them accordingly. When we both have a clear idea of everything that's involved in this problem, I'm sure we can formulate a solution.*

I don't want to hear any excuses.
Reply with:

☑ *And I don't have any to give you. What I'd like is some time to review the problems you have brought up and come back to you with some suggestions for solving them.*

You can't get away with sloppy work. I can't stand sloppy work.
Reply with:

☑ *I'm sorry that I've given you the feeling that I'm trying to get away with anything. Can we sit down and go over whatever problem areas you see? If I can get specifics, I can work with you on them one by one. Should I come back at a better time?*

Situation 1
Getting Hired

Volumes have been written on how to knock 'em dead at an interview. Unfortunately, unless you are an accomplished actor, it is virtually impossible to summon up the contents of these volumes when you're sitting across the desk from your potential employer. You'll find it more useful to prepare yourself for the interview with a few essential points:

Nobody enjoys interviewing job candidates.
Think your interviewer gets off on deciding the fate of the interviewee? Think again. Most executives regard interviewing job candidates as an intrusion into their routine, an unwelcome distraction. Most executives are uncomfortable during the interview. They feel that the candidate is judging *them* and judging the company through them. They are usually poorly prepared for the interview and at a loss for meaningful questions. Nor is the typical interviewer out to get you with trick questions or even particularly demanding questions. Interviewers do not want to create tension. Most job candidates go into an

interview as if it were an academic exam. It's nothing of the kind. In this case, you're almost certainly better prepared than the "examiner." With this in mind, rather than worry about potential questions and how you'll respond to them, think about issues *you* can raise at the interview. For example, prepare yourself by reviewing hot trends in the industry and bring these up in your interview. These are issues your interviewer should raise, but he almost certainly will not. The easier you make it on the interviewer, the more he'll like you and the better the impression you will make.

Keep it simple.
Think in terms of headlines. Resolve to make three, four, or five big points about yourself. Avoid adjectives but use plenty of nouns and verbs—which is another way of saying, don't *tell* the interviewer how he should feel about you, *show* him by enumerating your achievements and accomplishments. One of the first things a good writer learns to do is to show rather than tell. Try to do the same in an interview. Make your points with concrete words that summon up specific events and particular deeds. Outline these points in your mind before going into the interview. The candidate with whom the interviewer can associate a few positive facts has a decided advantage over the others.

Keep it positive.
Do not complain about your present position. Do not criticize management at your present position. Not "I'm bored where I'm at," but "I want a greater level of responsibility and challenge."

Prepare your vocabulary.

Words to Use

accomplishments	*efficient*
advise	*energetic*
anticipate	*evaluation*
awake	*goal*
aware	*improved*
built	*information*
consult	*initiated*
coordinate	*motivated*
coordinator	*profit*
corporate	*reevaluated*
created	*responsive*
earned	*revamped*

revised
revitalized
seek
self-starter
sensitive

started
success
successfully
team
teamwork

Phrases to Use

accept criticism
corporate image
eager to take on additional
*   responsibility*
extra effort
eyes open
for the first time
goal-oriented
head on

in touch
make use of criticism
management team
nothing stops me
take charge
take direction
team effort
walk through walls for this
*   job*

Words to Avoid

bad
bored
depressed
frustrated
hard

incompetent
slow
tired
trouble

Phrases to Avoid

dead end
didn't see eye to eye
disagreed with my boss
get away with
no future

terrible boss
too difficult
too easy
too many hours
too much work

Your Script

You: *The challenge I see in this position is knowing how to write lively, user-friendly prose without compromising the necessary technical depth. It's this kind of balancing act that keeps the job exciting.*

Interviewer: *Do you think you have the ability to write clear technical prose that won't put our customers to sleep?*

You: *I wouldn't waste your time if I weren't confident that I could do the job. I've been writing technical bulletins on a free-lance basis for three years now. I don't know if you've had a chance to take a look at the update I wrote for the QBX Terminal Emulation software, but I'm particularly proud of that. The challenge was to provide a concise, practical overview of a significantly revised software application. Roger Wilko at*

QBX was so pleased that he's asked me to take on the entire manual for the next full release of the software.

Interviewer: *Your present full-time position as a technical editor gives you time to take on free-lance work. You understand that a writing position with us wouldn't leave any time for free-lance work. In fact, it's against company policy.*

You: *I understand fully. Ms. Flint, my supervisor at WestTech, is aware that I do free-lance work. The salary range for the position you have available would make it unnecessary for me to take on additional work. In any case, part of the reason I've been doing free-lance work is personal satisfaction. Writing full-time here would give me all the job satisfaction I need. Incidentally, I'm confident that I could bring the QBX manual in-house here as a company project.*

Keep the interview substantive by raising key issues yourself. Do not depend on the interviewer to raise these issues. Remember, you are better prepared for the interview than he is. Be as specific as possible—substitute deeds for adjectives—but don't get into a complex discussion. Using specifics, make a few vivid points about your qualifications for the job. Keep the tone positive throughout, but try always to back your ample self-praise with concrete evidence.

Responses to Anticipate

Knocking off a few free-lance assignments is very different from doing this work every day.
Reply with:

☑ *I agree. But I certainly don't see the difference as a problem. I'm the kind of writer who thrives on regular hours. That's how I hit my stride and maintain it.*

I'm not sure we're right for you.
Reply with:

☑ *I appreciate your frankness and concern. All I can say is that I've taken a good close look at your company, and I've given a great deal of thought to the position. I am as sure as I can be that you're right for me, and I'm quite confident that you'll be pleased with the work I do for you.*

I'm going to put you on the spot. Tell me in a single sentence why I should hire you.
Reply with:

☑ *I innovate and I adapt.*

We're interviewing a good many people for this position, and it will take a few weeks to get back to you.
Reply with:

☑ *I've never been shy of competition, and I hope, during that time, you'll contact me if you have any further questions.*

Situation 2
Getting a Raise

In Arthur Miller's play *Death of a Salesman*, Uncle Charlie remarks, "No man ever has enough salary." You might as well begin by accepting that as a fact and stop worrying about whether you "deserve" a raise. You *need* one, and that's all there is to it. However, you should not put it to your boss that way.

What do you need a raise for? A new car? A new house? To hang on to the house you have? To send your kid to college? Depending on the kind of boss you work for, she may or may not personally care about your needs outside of the workplace. In either case, if she is doing her job, she will recognize those outside needs as irrelevant to deciding whether to give you a raise. After all, a dozen other people in the company want a new car or a new house, have a tough mortgage to meet and a son or daughter to send to college. Therefore, what you say to get yourself a raise has to be job-related and job-related only.

Actually, that makes things a lot easier, at least as far as your emotions are concerned. If it's hard enough to make a persuasive case for a raise based on your performance at work, think how much harder it would be if you had to justify your whole life. ("Why does *he* need a new car? *I* can't afford a new car. Why should I make it possible for him to buy one?" says your boss to herself.) So it is better, all the way around, to keep the discussion focused on how you meet (and exceed!) the demands of your job, on your professional performance, merit, and productivity.

Go into the discussion armed with two sets of facts: 1) a verbal resume that hits the highlights of the year's accomplishments and that reminds your boss of your duties, skills, and responsibilities; and

2) facts about what others, in similar jobs, get paid—assuming, of course, it's more than you get now.

So much for the information you should be certain to convey. You should also prepare yourself with some research you will keep in reserve, to use as needed. Be aware of how well (or poorly) your company performed during the past year. If your company issues an annual report, read it. Determine your worth on the job market; good sources for this information are compensation surveys published by trade organizations in your field. Determine, too, whether you are a person in short supply or if the market for your position is glutted. Based on this information and, of course, your present salary, you should be able to determine a reasonable range to shoot for, and, equally important, you'll have the information you need to back up your request to your boss.

Bear this in mind: You are not *asking* for a raise. You are *negotiating* for one. You are not a charity case, out to get something for nothing. You have valuable skills and experience to offer, for which you are trying to get the best price. As in any negotiation, you should not show all your cards at once. Have a firm idea of how much more money you can reasonably expect, but do not begin the discussion by stating a dollar amount. The potential problem is not that the number will be too high (and your boss will laugh in your face and you'll be humiliated, etc., etc., etc.), but that it will be too low. The best tactic is to elicit an offer and, depending on how that figure jives with what your research and desires tell you is appropriate, accept the offer or use it as the basis for further negotiation.

Words to Use

appropriate	*imaginative*
asset	*negotiate*
commitment	*performance*
committed	*productive*
creativity	*reasonable*
dedicated	*resourceful*
duties	*responsibilities*
fair	*valuable*
feasible	*workable*
imagination	

Phrases to Use

can we negotiate   *commitment to the company*
commitment to productivity

commitment to this
    department
cut costs
expanded territory
increased market
increased productivity

industry-standard
    compensation
not carved in stone
put in whatever hours are
    necessary

Words to Avoid

bored
cheated
demand
final
mismanagement

non-negotiable
tired
underpaid
unfair

Phrases to Avoid

cost of living
I can't afford
I demand
I insist
I'll have to quit
I'm overworked
I need
It seems to me that

others have advanced
that's my final word on the
    subject
this is not negotiable
you expect too much
you have to
you must

Your Script

    Thanks for seeing me, Mary [if you routinely use your boss's first name]. I've been with Reedim & Wheep for six years now—two years in sales, and the past four years in marketing. You know the quality of work I've been doing here. Since I took over the Lummocks account, we've penetrated two major new markets and at least one new territory—and the year's not over yet. Now I'm just starting on the Burdon account. It needs a lot of work, but I feel good about it, and I'm confident that I can do for Burdon what I've done for Lummocks.

    You've given me a lot of creative freedom, which is great, and I've assembled a terrific team: I'm supervising six people on the Lummocks account, and I'll be putting together eight on the Burdon job, at least at start-up. I've advanced pretty fast here, and I've had to take on a lot of responsibilities. I believe it's time that my salary caught up with my level of achievement and responsibilities. It's time that my salary got into step with industry-standard compensation.

    What do you think, Mary?

You have presented your case, hinted at a range ("industry-stand-

ard"), and now, rather than demand a "yes" or "no" to some amount
you propose, you place the matter in the hands of your boss. You've
demonstrated that your performance merits a certain level of compensation, and you've given your boss the very good feeling that she
is a fair person and a shrewd judge of talent and ability. You've set up
a context that makes it possible for your boss to respond positively.
You've also made it possible for your boss to make an offer. If all goes
well, the raise will, in effect, be *her* idea.

Responses to Anticipate

*If it were up to me, there's no question that you'd get a raise. I can
make a recommendation, but I'm essentially powerless to make the final decision.*

Reply with:

☑ *Whom should I talk to, then? And can I count on your recommendation to him or her?*

*To tell you the truth, a lot of people here are doing great jobs, and
they're not getting the kind of raise you're talking about.*

Reply with:

☑ *I'm only talking about myself and what is appropriate in my case.*

I can't offer you 15 percent. Five is more like it.

Reply with:

☑ *Say nothing, but don't leave. The silence will be awkward for both
of you, but you are in control. Your boss may become uncomfortable enough to make a better offer or, at least, initiate further negotiation.*

After the silence, your boss says, *I'm afraid that's final. Five percent
is as high as I can go.*

Reply with:

☑ *Okay, I'll work at that salary, provided that we have a firm understanding that in three months we will review what I've done and
where I've put the company. I'm committed to this job, and I'm
willing to wait the three months. (Be certain to follow this with a
memo that summarizes your understanding of the agreement.)*

I can't accommodate you at this time.
Reply with:

☑ *Is there something I've done or failed to do?*

Or:

☑ *What can I do to change your mind on this?*

Or:

☑ *Tell me what would make it possible for me to get more appropriate compensation.*

Situation 3
Getting a Promotion

Seeking a promotion is similar to negotiating for a raise in that your task is to sell your boss on your value, negotiating a deal rather than making a demand or asking for something in return for nothing. Indeed, in many cases it is more appropriate to seek a promotion than it is to ask for a raise. Many positions have formal or informal salary ceilings, and the next step up the compensation ladder is through a loftier position. Is it harder to get a raise or to get a promotion? That's the same kind of question as the classic posed to optimists and pessimists: Is the glass half-empty or half-full? The pessimist will tell you that it's harder to get a promotion because you are asking for two things, more money *and* more responsibility. By the same token, the pessimist might also tell you that it's harder to get a raise because you're asking for more money without doing anything more for it. An optimist, on the other hand, may opine that a boss is more likely to yield on money than on power. Or the optimist may tell you that a boss is more likely to tie a raise to a promotion because she feels she is getting a better bargain—paying more, but also getting more.

The pessimist/optimist debate may be useful for anticipating possible responses, but it is not worth much worry. End the debate by arbitrarily taking the optimist's position; warranted or not, it's the only viewpoint that will do you any good in a negotiation. If you have a choice between asking for a raise or asking for a promotion, begin by deciding what you want. Most people will choose the promotion, and if that's what you want, here is the best way to begin: You can—and should—take the position that you are offering to take on more responsibility in exchange for greater compensation. This not only has the potential for giving your boss positive feelings about parting with more money, even more important, it should allow you to feel less like a supplicant and more like a good businessperson. After all, you are not simply asking for more but offering value for value in a way that shows respect for yourself and a commitment to your company.

Even if you are turned down for the promotion, you are still in a position to negotiate a raise in your present position. If you had begun by asking for a raise, you would have had no definite, positive fallback position.

So regardless of how you may feel, go into the discussion not as one who is *asking* for something but as a businessperson with an offer to make. As with getting hired or securing a raise, it is far better to come into the discussion armed with a few solid accomplishments than with a canned spiel consisting of self-laudatory adjectives. The golden rule of writers applies to this negotiation as well: *show*, don't *tell*. Building on a base of accomplishment, suggest that you could be even more useful in a position of greater responsibility.

For most of us, it is emotionally very difficult to *ask* for things. It is also true that most people would rather receive than give. Therefore, secure your promotion by offering rather than asking.

Words to Use

accomplished	*knowledge*
achieved	*manage*
capable	*management*
create	*motivation*
do	*objectives*
established	*offer*
expand	*opportunity*
expedite	*our*
experience	*overview*
formulated	*perspective*
goals	*potential*
ideas	*resources*
imagination	*responsibility*
improve	*skill*
innovate	*solve*
judgment	*talent*

Phrases to Use

able to make decisions	*big picture*
achieved goals	*both sides of the desk*
better suited	*command decisions*

from bottom to top
gained experience
invaluable experience
make better use of
management team
more flexibility
our company
our department
our mission

overall view
problem solver
problem solving
seen both sides
shirtsleeves manager
team effort
team player
time-tested judgment
willing to take charge

Words to Avoid

ask
beg
bored
boss
brass

increase
need
raise
sluggish
wasted

Phrases to Avoid

bored to death
can't stand it
*don't know what to do with
    myself*
eager beaver
it's about time
it's only fair

no future in it
no challenge
or else
take it or leave it
that's the way it is
wasted down there

Your Script

I've been on the selling floor now for just about four years. Three out of those four years I've been among your top three salesmen. I have learned a lot here—not only about selling shoes, but about what sells and what does not. I've also learned that I have a lot to offer—and not just on a customer-by-customer basis. I know that Mr. Grimaldi is moving up from assistant buyer. I'm ready to move up to working more closely with you. I've had a long and successful record of customer contact, but I've been concentrating as much on the product as on the customers. I've got a very fresh perspective on what is selling here—what moves, what doesn't, and what we need—and I'd like to put that to work for us as our new assistant buyer. And since I like this company and want to stay with this company, well, I'd like the opportunity to learn—to take what I know and develop it. This is my career.

The most important point to note here is how the applicant turns a request into an offer. He states the facts and establishes his credentials and record of good work—not toward the end of proving that he "deserves" a promotion, but with the goal of selling his additional services to the company. If I was good doing x, think how much more I could do for you if I were doing y. You don't have to sell your boss on the fact that a promotion will benefit you. She knows that. Your task is to sell her on the idea that promoting you will greatly benefit the company and, therefore, her. The applicant goes on to establish his commitment to the firm, acknowledges that he will not rest in the new position, and declares that he is willing and eager to continue to learn. There is a fine line between exuding confidence and coming off as overbearing and arrogant. Not only do bosses find arrogance obnoxious, many are threatened by it. You do not want to give your boss the message that you are gunning for her job. You *do* want to give her the message that promoting you will make her look better.

Responses to Anticipate

I don't think you are ready yet.
Reply with:

☑ *What will it take for me to demonstrate that I am ready?*

This is not the right time to talk about it.
Reply with:

☑ *When would be a better time? Can you pencil me in now?*

You're doing such a good job where you're at, that I'm afraid to move you out of the position.
Reply with:

☑ *Well, it sure is nice to be appreciated, but I'm confident that I can take the same skills and use them to greater advantage in a more responsible position. I want to contribute as much as possible to our department.*

I need to keep you where you're at for at least another year.
Reply with:

☑ *I'd like to schedule a review before that time, to discuss my progress and my prospects. Can we plan on that now?*

We're planning to fill that position with somebody from the outside.
Reply with:

☑ *Is that final and set in stone? What would it take to change your mind? (. . . to change company policy?) I'm committed to this company, and I want a stake in its future. Can you tell me what it would take to get me in the running for this promotion?*

Situation 4
Promoting an Idea or Project

This situation presents more variables than most others, since the nurturing and reception of ideas and projects are subject to the vagaries of a variety of corporate psychologies. Some bosses welcome and encourage innovation, while others subtly or even actively discourage it.

This book began by suggesting that before you attempt to speak up to an authority figure, you should deliberately try to imagine the worst that can happen to you. Usually the exercise will demonstrate that the worst is not so bad. In the case of promoting a new idea or project, the response may be very gratifying indeed—pats on the back and encouragement—or, at the other extreme, you may be met with outright hostility, discouragement, and derision. The phrase that usually applies is "shot down": *He shot me down. I was shot down.* Or even, *I went down in flames.* The vividness of the metaphor suggests the strength of the bad feelings associated with fear of rejection and humiliation.

If you happen to work in a corporate environment where innovation is discouraged, nothing I can suggest here will greatly affect your reality. If the opportunity for creativity and innovation is important to you, perhaps you should think about moving to an emotionally healthier company that welcomes these qualities. In the meantime, however, try to remember two things when you promote an idea or program.

First, if your boss habitually rejects innovation, *he's* the one with a problem. He may make *you* feel bad, but he's the one in really bad shape. Rejection of innovation—or, more precisely, preemption of the mere discussion of innovation—is a sign of a very unhealthy manager. Unfortunately, your boss's illness also becomes your problem, but at least it may give you some comfort to bear in mind that, by thinking, evaluating, and proposing, you are doing the healthy and desirable thing.

Second, unpleasant as rejection can be, it is not really as painfully final as that "shot down" figure of speech suggests. I do not mean to minimize the bad feelings that derision and rejection produce, but they are, after all, only feelings. Don't give them the con-crete reality of a fiery death in aerial combat. Yes, promoting an idea or project to an unhealthy boss may result in your feeling bad, but you will not actually burst into flame. And if you are working for a com-pany where innovation can seriously threaten your job, well, it is high time you moved on.

Bearing in mind that this situation presents a broad range of pos-sible responses depending on varied corporate psychology, my sug-gestions are based on best-case and worst-case scenarios.

In the best case—promoting an idea or project to a boss who generally welcomes creativity—begin by preparing as thoroughly as possible. The presentation, of course, can range from a lengthy pro-posal prepared in accordance with prescribed company policy to a spur-of-the-moment remark at a meeting. At either extreme, prepara-tion is possible—and essential. When you present your boss with a ream of lovingly prepared research papers, try to say three or four things.

1. *"Here's the proposal for"*—and then be as specific about the name of the project as possible.

2. *"As you look through the proposal, you might want to take special note of"*—then list a small number of *specific* highlights or is-sues.

3. *"I'm especially concerned about*—whatever—*and I'm anxious to get your take on it."*

4. *"It's been very exciting to work on this, and I'd appreciate all the feedback I can get from you."* (That is, convey your enthusiasm and let your boss know how much you value his response.)

The spur-of-the-moment remark should also be the product of some preparation, even at companies where you are encouraged to shoot from the hip. Brief yourself on the agenda of the meeting, and arm yourself with notes. When you present an idea, you might pref-ace it with a phrase like, "This is something that just occurred to me," or "Here's something I think would be worth further thought," or "I just had a thought that might bear working up." It is also a good idea to ask your boss or those assembled at the meeting for help: "Help me out with this one," or "What do you think about," "What's your quick take on," and so on.

These steps also apply in the worst-case scenario, but you need to augment them with a strategy that seeks to give your boss a manifest stake in your idea or project. You need to make your boss see himself as your partner in the project. For example, modify point #2 above by saying something like, "As you look through the proposal, you might want to take special note of how I incorporated your thoughts in . . . " or, ". . . what I did with the concepts you and I discussed last month." In point #3, put even more weight on the importance of the boss's response: "I'd really be grateful for help with such and such," or "Such and such needs a lot more work. I need your take on it." Make point #4 a team statement: "It was great working with you on this," and so on.

Is such sentiment genuine? Are you kidding? But making a resistant boss your partner may well be your only shot at selling the idea or project. Swallow hard, and don't be shy about being manipulative in a good cause.

Words to Use

advice	plan
care	planning
careful	potential
effective	profitable
exciting	prudent
experience	revise
expertise	special
help	tested
innovative	wisdom

Phrases to Use

given a great deal of thought to	sink our teeth into
improve the bottom line	take the upside
I need your advice	the intelligent way to
I need your take on	trial period
I think you'll find	try something new
minimum risk	user-friendly
opens up possibilities	very excited about this
reaction has been good	win-win situation
really run with	without risk
run all the numbers	you will appreciate

Words to Avoid

afraid	experiment
backward	fear

guarantee | risk
nervous | should
panic | stodgy

Phrases to Avoid

give it a shot | take a chance
might work | take a flier
risk-adverse | take a risk for a change
set in our ways | what can go wrong?
should work | what the hell?
spirit of adventure

Your Script

I'm very excited that I've finished the prospectus for the travel-book series I mentioned to you the week before last. And here it is. The potential I think you'll see in it is a combination of a fresh approach to a tested market and all the advantages of a series—a single design, a single format, a proven stable of authors, but a potentially unlimited number of titles. You'll find that I've run all the numbers here, and I'm confident you'll like what you see. I've given this one a lot of thought, but I could really use your take on format and size. This is one we can really run with.

Communicate your enthusiasm and attempt to shape the desired degree of receptiveness, but don't bully ("You're out of your mind if you don't go for this"). Concisely underscore the highlights of the proposal, giving specifics rather than adjectives; objective features rather than subjective attributes. Solicit your boss's input to get him on your team.

Responses to Anticipate

This one looks like a tough sell to me. I just don't know.
Reply with:

☑ *You and I know they're all tough sells. What I ask is that you look over the proposal and look over the figures—then let me know how tough it is. I'll trust your take on it.*

I can't get to this for a while.
Reply with:

☑ *I know you're busy here. But I'm confident you'll be excited by what you see in the proposal. It's worth making time for.*

I'm putting all new projects on hold.
Reply with:

☑ *Even if you are, I'm so excited about this one that I'd really like to get your reaction to it and your advice on it—even if we can't act on it immediately.*

We need to move cautiously. I don't want to rush into anything.
Reply with:

☑ *Neither do I. That's why I've taken time with the proposal, and that's why I don't want to hurry it by you. I really need to get your response to it. Then I'll give it the time for all the revision and re-thinking it may need.*

Situation 5
Extending a Deadline

Bosses, even decent and understanding bosses, hate excuses, and nothing occasions more excuses than missing a deadline—failing to have a report ready in time, failing to finish a project by the due date. You might be able to get your boss to accept your excuse, but you will never be able to get her to like it. Therefore, it is better to make no excuses.

This does not mean that you ignore the problem or fail to inform your boss of an anticipated or unavoidable delay. Instead, recognize that extending a deadline is buying time, and like anything else you might purchase, the buying of time is subject to negotiation. Persuade your boss to sell you more time in exchange for value received. "To do the most thorough job possible on this, I'm going to need a week more. I don't think it will do us any good to try to rush it and end up neglecting x, y, and z." Instead of whining about not having enough time, make it clear what the additional time will buy—in this case, a more thorough, successful job.

It is always better to advise your boss in advance of a time problem. No one likes to feel backed into a corner. Moreover, showing that you are aware of the schedule demonstrates that, even as you are slipping a deadline, you are still in control. Try to recast the problem with the deadline as a simple alteration in schedule, not as a crisis caused by your being late. Avoid words like *due*, and substitute something like *scheduled for*. Do not suggest that the deadline is carved in stone, but that it is just one part of a continuum produced by human beings and subject to alteration by human beings.

Finally, as in any negotiation, offer as many alternatives as possible. "I can get *x* done by Wednesday, *y* by Friday, and *z* early next week." Or, "If I postpone *x*, I can get you *y* and *z* by the original deadline."

Words to Use

alter	*investigate*
aware	*management*
better	*methodically*
can	*modify*
care	*possible*
careful	*priorities*
caution	*reschedule*
expedite	*resources*
if	*will*

Phrases to Use

adjust our priorities	*do the job that should be done*
apportion our resources	
best job possible	*get this done more efficiently*
by the book	
cover ourselves thoroughly	*in order to*
do a creditable job	*manage our resources*
do a more thorough job	*pour on the steam*

Words to Avoid

cannot	*no*
crisis	*problem*
delay	*slipped*
due	*trouble*
forgot	*unaware*
impossible	*unreasonable*
late	

Phrases to Avoid

back burner	*it got by me*
before you know it	*it slipped past me*
big trouble	*my fault*
I forgot	*out of the question*
I'm late	*quick and dirty*
I'm sorry I'm late	*time flies*

Your Script

I need to talk to you about altering the schedule for the Smith pro-ject. All parts of the marketing report are scheduled for completion by May 15. I have enough information now to complete parts one through four by then, but a really thorough job on parts five and six is going to require an additional week of research. I don't see any point to just throw-ing this together. With a week's more time I can do the job the way it should be done, and we'll have a document we can reasonably base de-cisions on.

The speaker here communicates control and the sense that altering a schedule is perfectly routine rather than something one does in a hopeless emergency. The speaker offers alternatives that make this a progress report rather than a failure-to-progress report.

Responses to Anticipate

This is a serious deadline. I suggest that you move heaven and earth to meet it.

Reply with:

☑ *I take the deadline very seriously. That's why I'm talking to you about it now. I can give you a job I'm 75 percent happy with by the deadline. If I have another week, I can promise 100 percent. The deadline's serious, but so is the project.*

How are you guys spending your time down there?

Reply with:

☑ *One thing we're doing is thinking through the nature of the pro-ject and just how best to use our resources. If we cut corners now, it will cost us time later. That's why I'm asking for the modifica-tion of the schedule—to build a solid foundation at this point so that we don't have trouble further on. That's my judgment on the matter, and that's what I'm asking for.*

Can't you move any faster?

Reply with:

☑ *Certainly. But I'm not going to be comfortable with the results, and if I'm not comfortable, I can't expect you to be confident.*

Can you guarantee that this will be the last delay?
Reply with:

☑ *I can guarantee that we'll do everything possible to ensure that the schedule won't have to be altered again. We've built in some time to handle the unexpected—but if we get nothing but the unexpected, well, I'd be lying to you if I said I could guarantee no further changes. Give me the time I'm asking for, and you and I can be very reasonably confident that we'll not only meet the revised schedule, but meet it with a product that works.*

Situation 6
Accepting an Assignment

How you accept an assignment is a lot like how you shake hands. It is an initial act of communication that can convey far more than is at first apparent. A handshake is a chance to convey strength, warmth, eagerness, loyalty, a willingness to get the job done. Grip too firmly, and you convey the insecurity of one who feels it necessary to demonstrate dominance. Proffer your hand limply, and you convey weakness and hesitation. The way in which you accept an assignment presents similar opportunities and potential hazards.

To begin with, if you happen to be genuinely thrilled with the assignment, go ahead and express your feelings. It will give your boss pleasure to know that he has assigned you something you are excited about doing. It will also give him the feeling that he has chosen the right person for the job.

But what if you are less than thrilled with the task? Before you react, you must make an important decision. Do you have a choice as to whether you will accept the assignment? If you are in a position to decline, and that is what you wish to do, read "Situation 7: Declining an Assignment." If, however, you decide that you have no choice, it is still not necessary to counterfeit joy. What you do need to convey is the message that you will work enthusiastically and professionally to get the job done. Generally, this is all you *should* convey, and you should do so without qualification. But what if you have genuine, well-founded reservations about the assignment? What if you sincerely believe the project is doomed to fail? In such cases, you should neither feign enthusiastic confidence nor respond with panic-stricken negativity. Respond positively, but mention that you'll be back with some questions: "I'll start looking it over right away and be back to you with some questions and issues tomorrow." Give yourself time to review the pros and cons, the benefits and pitfalls of the project before you commit yourself to a definitive response. It is perfectly appropriate to buy time in this case, and it is certainly preferable to boxing yourself in with a thoughtlessly overconfident response on the one hand, or a rejection of the project on the other. Even if you ultimately demonstrate the unfeasibility of an assignment, you will have still succeeded in conveying your willingness to have engaged the task.

Words to Use

able

accept

acknowledge

agree

approve

armed

confidence

confident

delighted

enthusiastic

equipped

excited

experience

gratifying

great

opportunity

pleasant

pleased

prepared

studied

thrilled

willing

wonderful

workable

Phrases to Use

by all means

can count on me

give me a day to review the assignment

I look forward to working on this

I look forward to working with you

I know you'll be pleased with the result

I'll be back to you with some questions

I'll get on it immediately

I'm going to enjoy this

I'm pleased

I've been preparing for this

thank you for asking me

thank you for this opportunity

this is great

this will be fun

with great pleasure

you can count on me

you can rely on me

Words to Avoid

can't

doubt

fail

frightened

nervous

refuse

reject	*unworkable*
unqualified	

Phrases to Avoid

can't do it	*not overjoyed by this*
doesn't thrill me	*not something I'm good at*
doubt it will work	*not sure*
haven't got the experience	*not sure I'm qualified*
have too many doubts	*not up to it*
I'll do the best I can	*rather not*
I'll do what has to be done	*this is not my strong suit*
I've never tried this before	*you've got the wrong man*
lack the experience	*(woman)*

Your Script

1.

This is a very exciting opportunity. I've been preparing for just this kind of assignment, and I'll get on it immediately. I'm confident that you'll find my performance top-notch.

2.

I'm prepared to get this under way now, and I know that you will be pleased with the results.

3.

I'm very pleased that you've given this one to me. I've been wanting to work more closely with you on something—and now I have the opportunity. I look forward to it.

4.

I'll look this over right away, and I should be back to you with some questions and issues over the next day or two.

All of these responses are aimed at communicating enthusiasm and commitment that assure the boss that he has made the right choice.

Responses to Anticipate

Don't let your enthusiasm run away with you.
Reply with:

☑ *I run with my enthusiasm. It's what drives me.*

I'm counting on you.
Reply with:

☑ *I know you are, and I won't let you down.*

Are you sure you're up to this?
Reply with:

☑ *You are making the right choice. I've prepared for this kind of assignment, I'm thrilled to get it, and I will make it work.*

You seem to have some doubts.
Reply with:

☑ *What I have are some questions, and I need a day to review the assignment, formulate those questions, and come back to you with them.*

I'd like to see more enthusiasm.
Reply with:

☑ *I'm the careful sort. I need to look things over before I let myself get too excited. I'll review the assignment immediately and come back to you with any questions I have.*

Situation 7
Declining an Assignment

This far into *Speaking Up*, you might as well admit that you are reading (and I'll confess that I am writing) a—ugh!—Self-Help Book. One thing all such books are supposed to have in common is the unalterable conviction that life is a matter of choices and that you always have a choice. In philosophical terms, this is, in fact, true. You can decline any assignment, any time. For better or worse, however, ours is not a world of philosophers. In practical terms, the sad fact is, you do *not* always have a choice.

Just how much leeway you have is something only you can judge at a given time and in a given situation. One rule of thumb is generally applicable, however. If you are uncertain about an assignment, or even if you are certain you want to decline it, under most circumstances it is better to avoid an immediate negative response. Impale yourself on the horns of a dilemma—where a "yes" or "no" is required on the spot—and you are likely to make a bad decision. Instead, follow the advice of the preceding chapter: Say that you will review the assignment and that you will come back with any questions. After you have reviewed the assignment, assuming that you are in a practical position to make the choice, decline.

There are three ways to turn down an assignment. You may attack the assignment itself, demonstrating that the project is flawed, unfeasible, or unnecessary. Or you may argue that, while the project is fine, you are not the best choice for it, either because of lack of qualifications, lack of experience, or because you are a resource better used elsewhere. Finally, you may simply say that you prefer not to take on the project. Each of these approaches has advantages and dangers, and again, only you, operating at a given time in a given situation with a given boss, can determine which approach is most appropriate. However, some general guidelines are in order.

If you can demonstrate that a project is unworkable, you stand to save yourself as well as your company a lot of grief. But be strongly cautioned that the "if" here is a very big one. You should not protest the unworkability of an assignment just because you don't want to undertake it. This will benefit neither you nor your firm. Indeed, such action will, before long, earn you a well-deserved reputation as negative, uncooperative, evasive, even lazy. If, however, you are truly convinced that a project is doomed, present your well-reasoned doubts to your boss. "I mentioned that I'd be coming back to you on this project with some questions. I've reviewed the assignment, and, in fact, a number of very sticky points have come up. We'd better discuss and resolve these before we try to get this under way." Note the transition from "I" to "we." The message is not, "Boy, *you* have really stuck *me* with a turkey." Rather, the new equation is, "*I* have reviewed *the* project and have discovered that *we* have problems." As in any situation where you are delivering a negative, avoid an opposition of *I* against *you*. Instead, recruit your boss onto the team with *we*. Don't let a negative situation turn you and your boss into adversaries. Neither of you can afford that relationship.

It is also important to avoid simply tossing the job back into your boss's lap or to make him feel as if you are shooting *him* down. It is one thing to criticize a project vigorously if you have been specifically asked to evaluate it. However, if your task was not evaluation but execution, you can safely assume that your boss thinks the assignment a good one and will be, to some degree at least, protective of it. Any attempt to drive a stake through the heart of the idea will undoubtedly jab at the boss's ego, and that will get you nowhere—or worse. For this reason, frame your criticism as positively as possible. This does not mean that you should be patronizing but that, instead of rejecting the project out of hand, you should point out that there are "questions," "loose ends," "problems," "sticking points," and so on that need to be "resolved before proceeding." This indicates that you are still engaged with the project. It also gives your boss an opportunity to acknowledge the difficulties for himself, rather than have you humiliatingly force the recognition of them upon him. If the problems are formidable enough, the project will die—or it will be modified, made workable, and perhaps even become a feasible, tolerable, enjoyable assignment you can freely accept.

What if there is nothing wrong with the project, but you are convinced that it is not right for you or, more to the point, you are not right for it? The object here is to get your boss to see things your way in this *particular* case without prompting him to question your competence generally. Circumstances permitting, the safest course is to convince him that you are a resource better used on a different project. Unfortunately, another project has to be currently available before you can use this strategy. If this strategy is unavailable to you, do not blurt out your lack of qualifications, but begin the process of declining the assignment by securing time to review it, promising to return with questions. When you return, try to come armed with alternatives: "I've reviewed the project, and it seems to me that somebody in Special Sales would be better positioned to take this on. More than half the project depends on direct mail." If possible, rather than directing attention to your unsuitability, focus on the alternative. Your boss is primarily interested in getting the job done, not in getting *you* to do the job. If you simply say that you are not particularly qualified for the assignment, what your boss hears is that the job will not be getting done. If, however, you nominate someone else for the assignment, it is true that you are still bowing out, but doing so will not leave the task an orphan.

And if there is no alternative?

Then you must proceed with caution. The best thing you can do in this case is to make a demonstration of frankness and mature self-evaluation. If you were accepting an assignment, you would do well to bring up some recent past success to suggest that you can achieve the same results now. In declining an assignment, you may also want to bring up a past success, first to suggest your general competence (the present assignment is a rare instance for which you are not the right choice) and, second, to contrast the kinds of strengths previously demonstrated with what the present assignment calls for. "As you are aware, I did so well with the Baker account because I know widgets backwards and forwards. The project you've asked me to take demands that same level of familiarity with framisses. I've got to be frank with you: I just don't know framisses."

Finally, it is possible that your work situation permits you sufficient leeway simply to turn down an assignment at will. Even in this case, it's best to try to offer alternatives and to have a good reason for declining an assignment. It is always a good idea to frame your rejection in terms of doing what's best for the company. "I'd like to take a pass on this one. Somebody like Fredericks can take this kind of thing and really run with it. I'm better at the conceptual end. The project will move faster with someone who's got this stuff down cold."

Words to Use

alternatives	*priorities*
balance	*problems*
best	*qualified*
better	*questions*
consider	*reconsider*
difficulties	*resolve*
effective	*resource*
evaluate	*review*
experienced	*snags*
hurdles	*strength*
idea	*think*
manage	*time*
management	*value*
obstacles	*weigh*

Phrases to Use

best for the company	*questions to answer*
best for the project	*reevaluate priorities*
best for the team	*serious considerations*
best use of resources	*sink my teeth into*
consider the alternatives	*stronger in this area*
cost in resources	*take the ball and run with it*
cost in time	*take time to weigh*
difficulties to work out	*team player*
do it right	*think this through*
know I'll have questions	*time to evaluate*
play to my strengths	*time to review*
problems to resolve	

Words to Avoid

can't	*ridiculous*
impossible	*tired*
incapable	*waste*
mistaken	*won't*
overburdened	*worthless*
overloaded	

Phrases to Avoid

afraid to do it	*I'm overloaded*
beyond me	*impossible to do*
can't ask me to do	*incapable of*
something like this	*just don't have the*
can't imagine how I could	*qualifications for*
do it	*unreasonable demand on me*
cannot do it	*waste of time*
don't want to do it	*worn out*
I can't do any more	*wrong-headed*

Your Script

1.

I've reviewed the project we discussed, and, as I thought, it raises a lot of questions. There are some formidable hurdles we'll have to consider before we get under way. I'd like to go over them with you one by one.

2.

After thinking this assignment through, I've reached the conclusion that I'm not the most effective choice to get the job done as efficiently as possible. Half the work is technical analysis—the really important half. I'm much better at market analysis, and in order to get this project on track, that's the part of the job I should be doing. Have you talked to Benjamin or Von Humboldt? They've got the technical side of this down cold, and we would save a lot of time using them.

3.

I've looked at this thoroughly, and I'd like to take a pass on it. It's not the kind of assignment I can really sink my teeth into. I've got some alternatives to suggest, however.

All of these responses have one thing in common: they decline without rejecting. It is not just a matter of bowing out gracefully, but of providing alternatives that assure your boss that the project is not in peril.

Responses to Anticipate

I really want you to do this.
Reply with:

☑ *I would be glad to do it, if I didn't think there were people here who could do it more effectively. I strongly feel that my taking on this assignment would not be the best use of our resources.*

How can you turn something like this down?
Reply with:

☑ *It isn't easy, and I'm grateful for the confidence you've shown in me. That's why I'd like us to sit down and review the project once more. Until we've addressed the issues I've mentioned, I can't in good conscience tell you that I can accomplish what we both want from this assignment.*

I'm not accustomed to being turned down like this.
Reply with:

☑ *I'm not turning you down. I'm just suggesting that you reconsider your choice for this assignment.*

Situation 8
Taking a Compliment

Nothing should be easier. Your boss says something nice to you. You thank her. And you're both happy. End of story.

Well, for many of us, not quite the end.

If you have a hard time taking a compliment, you're not alone. It's a problem for many of us, who have been admonished from an early age to be "modest" because nobody likes a bragger. People who are too full of themselves, we are told, look foolish and, sooner or later, fall flat on their faces. The truth is that such injunctions against feeling good about our accomplishments never breed true modesty, but instead make us seem graceless and ungrateful when we are complimented or given some form of positive recognition. Learning how to accept a compliment gracefully can overcome the ingrained taboos of childhood and let us claim our just desserts not only with poise and dignity but with generosity to ourselves and to the person who gave the compliment. How you take a compliment is not only an opportunity to feel good, it is also a chance to make your boss feel good by giving her the pleasure of having bestowed recognition where it is deserved. Taking a compliment with appropriate grace will give your boss the satisfying feeling that she has acted rightly and is wise in placing confidence in you.

The simplest way to accept a compliment is simply to say "thank you." If you add something like, "Coming from you, that really means something," you have a perfectly adequate response. However, you might want to use the occasion to build additional goodwill and good feeling between you and your boss. Why not take the compliment as you might accept some award that is being presented to you? With this in mind, you might think about what people do when they get an award, and apply the example to your situation:

- Express pleasure.
- Express surprise, even shock, if the compliment really is unexpected.
- Express your regard for your boss.
- Convey a sense of modesty—but don't overdo it. Leave your boss convinced that her compliment is deserved.
- Share the praise with others who deserve it, naming names; recognize your colleagues and coworkers.

While you're at it, you might think about the kinds of stupid things people say when they get an award. Avoid the following:

- Don't "confess" unworthiness. It is ungenerous to yourself and even less generous to the person who pays you the compliment.
- Don't deliver a long speech; don't start acknowledging every last person with whom you have ever come into contact.

Words to Use

accept	generous
acknowledge	goodwill
amazed	grateful
delighted	gratified
deserved	happy
faith	help
firm	kind
flabbergasted	pleased
generosity	pleasure

positive
pride
proud
recognition
reward
source
strength
support

thank
thankful
thrilled
unexpected
unstinting
untiring
wonderful

Phrases to Use

approval from someone I
    respect
bowled over
feel so good
give full credit to
greatest admiration

great pleasure
highest regard
pleasure to work with
received plenty of support
you have been so
    generous/kind

Words to Avoid

embarrassed
luck
mistake

silly
undeserved
unworthy

Phrases to Avoid

I really don't deserve this
it was a piece of cake
it was easy
it was nothing
I was just lucky

save your compliments
there was nothing to it
think nothing of it
you shouldn't say such
    things

Your Script

Boss: *I want to tell you that I think you've handled Perkins's complaint very intelligently. That was good work.*

You: *Thank you. Coming from you, that's a real compliment. If there's one thing I've learned working in this department, it's to put the customer first. You've taught us to be good listeners, and that's the first step in customer relations.*

Accept a compliment by giving a compliment—not just thanks. *A compliment from you is something of real value.* Or: *You've helped me achieve what I have achieved.* From such an exchange of bouquets, both you and your boss emerge with good feelings.

Responses to Anticipate

You deserve it.

Reply with:

☑ *I've had a good example set for me. You've given me a lot of support.*

Don't be modest.

Reply with:

☑ *And I thought I was being pretty obnoxious!*

I don't give praise lightly.

Reply with:

☑ *I know you don't. That's why I'm so pleased that you like what I've done. It means a great deal to me.*

Situation 9
Taking Your Lumps

Okay, so *some* of us have trouble taking compliments. *All* of us have even more trouble taking criticism. This chapter does not concern criticism incurred for accidents and errors—these get a chapter of their own—but more general negative comments on performance or some other aspect of your work. We have to begin by acknowledging that any criticism you receive from your boss is just plain scary, even if it is delivered with some degree of sensitivity. Moreover, the object of this chapter is *not* to show you how to let such criticism "roll off your back," but how to respond to the criticism in a genuinely useful manner. The assumption is that such a response will not only go a long way toward keeping you from feeling paralyzed or devastated, but it will also compel you to deal with the criticism. For you should *not* let criticism roll off your back. You should not armor yourself against it. You should not ignore it. Negative though it is, you should accept criticism as an opportunity.

How?

Please entertain the following notion: All criticism, even unmerited criticism, is useful to you.

How?

- On the most basic, practical level, criticism may actually point out things you are doing ineffectively or poorly, things you could do better. Anybody doing a job requires feedback in order to fine-tune the work. Fight the impulse to fend off criticism. Listen to it. Learn from it.

- Even unmerited criticism offers opportunities for learning. Criticism is a perception, nothing more. Objective measurements—sales figures, for example—may indicate that you are doing a very good job, yet your boss may find something to criticize. Does this mean your boss is wrong or an ungrateful jerk? Quite possibly. But that conclusion should not prompt you to ignore the criticism. Explore, with yourself and with your boss, the reasons behind the criticism. Can you do something that will maintain the excellent sales performance you have achieved while also allowing your boss to *perceive* that you are doing a good job? This is not to say that you should meekly accept unjust or unfounded criticism (we will discuss responses shortly), but you should not simply throw it away like so much trash. Even misguided criticism is useful to you.

- Finally, criticism—accurate or unfounded—gives you an opportunity to respond, to communicate in a way that can strengthen and enhance your relationship with your boss.

As much as it may hurt, then, *listen* to criticism. Equally important, *demonstrate* that you are listening. This requires conscious awareness and, if necessary, adjustment of your body language. Make and maintain eye contact with your boss. This may be difficult—not because of you, but because of your boss. Some bosses, it is true, enjoy criticizing employees. Others derive genuine satisfaction from teaching, from helping to bring about development and improvement. Still others simply enjoy domination and tyranny. More bosses, however, are very uncomfortable delivering criticism, and, for this reason, tend to avoid eye contact. You should also be wary of the signals of resistance you may be giving. The most common are a hand placed over the mouth or on the forehead as if to shade—and partially conceal— the eyes, or arms folded across the chest. Such gestures are powerful signals of resistance that tell your boss you are determined *not* to hear her. In general, it is best that both you and your boss be seated during the discussion, since standing suggests and promotes face-to-face confrontation. If you must stand, it is best to keep your hands at your sides and to avoid the temptation to put your arms akimbo. This suggests defiance and sends a provocative message.

Why be so careful and conscious about these things? You want to take advantage of an opportunity to demonstrate your willingness to listen, to learn, to change, and to cooperate. You are not rolling over and playing dead; you are demonstrating your openness, which is a way of suggesting self-confidence rather than defiance or defensiveness. This will sound perverse, but it is infinitely to your advantage to make criticizing you an easy and rewarding experience for your boss.

Words to Use

advice	helpful
advise	helps
appreciate	improve
change	input
convert	pointers
correct	redo
effective	revamp
efficient	revise
encourage	revitalize
encouraging	rework
future	right
grateful	thanks

Phrases to Use

by all means	it would help me
from now on	more effective
get your input	more efficient
give this a trial	move forward
good point	next time
happy to try it your way	this is helpful
helps me see	well-founded
I appreciate	you have a good point
in the future	your advice is welcome

Words to Avoid

blame	poor
dumb	turf
fail	unfair
fault	unreasonable
inadequate	

Phrases to Avoid

can't be done	give me a break
get off my case	I can't

I'm only human   *won't try it*
this is unfair   *won't work that way*
What do you expect?   *wrong way*

Your Script

1.

BOSS: *I don't want to run you down, but you should have been able to process those orders faster. You need to delegate responsibility more effectively.*

You: *I appreciate what you are saying, and I would be grateful for any advice you can give me on how to expedite these kinds of orders. I'm open to suggestion. I'd like to see the orders get out of here faster myself.*

2.

BOSS: *I have not been entirely pleased with the quality of the work coming out of your department. I want to talk to you about it.*

You: *I wasn't aware of any problem. By all means, let's talk. I want to get your input. If you can show me what needs improvement, I'll move heaven and earth to make the changes.*

3.

BOSS: *You've got some big-time problems here. A 4-percent reject rate is just too high, and I won't tolerate it.*

You: *I'm aware of the problem, and I'd like to sit down and talk to you about it. I want to hear what you've got to say, and then I'll tell you how I plan to make improvements. It would be very helpful to get your opinion on the steps I plan to take.*

Your boss may well be spoiling for confrontation. Your best verbal strategy is to avoid confrontation without, however, evading it. Engage the issue rather than the personality. You may feel hurt and threatened. Ride out those feelings rather than act on them. Engage the issue, and invite your boss to *sit down* and talk (not lecture or admonish or harangue, but talk).

Responses to Anticipate

You'd better shape up here.
Reply with:

☑ *I've listened to your observations, and I need to review the problems you've pointed out. I'll come back to you with a plan that addresses these difficulties.*

Generally, you do a fine job. But I hope that you can show improvement in the areas we discussed.
Reply with:

☑ *You've been very helpful, and I'm confident that the problems you've noted can be resolved.*

I hope you don't feel I'm picking on you.
Reply with:

☑ *This kind of "picking" I can use. I need all the feedback I can get. Frankly, I don't agree with everything you've said, but you have given me a lot to think about. I'll review my methods and make some changes I think you will like.*

I want to see real, significant improvement.
Reply with:

☑ *So do I. I need to reflect on the situation for a bit. My initial reaction is that you are overstating the degree of the problem. But I do agree that my department can perform at a higher level, and I will do everything possible to achieve that level. I appreciate your input, and we will do better.*

Situation 10
Accidents and Errors

As I suggested in the preceding section, good or bad, just about everything that happens in the office is an opportunity for communication, which can build a better relationship between you and your boss. I'm not saying that you should jump up and down and cheer when you make a mistake or an accident befalls you. Mistakes and accidents are not good. True, they are usually not as bad as you think they are at the moment, but the fact is that *some* are even worse than they at first appear. Some can cost you your job. If you are dealing in life and death—if you are a policeman, a physician, a structural engineer, a bus driver—some accidents and errors can be fatal. No degree of good communications skills can alter that.

I am not suggesting an escape from reality, but I am recommending that you embrace probability. *Most* mistakes and accidents in and of themselves are not fatal or beyond repair. Too often, however, the feelings such incidents generate *are* destructive—even more destructive than the event itself. Effective communications can minimize such damaging results and, in many cases, even produce positive feelings. For what all accidents and errors offer in common is the divine opportunity for forgiveness. It is a fact that most of us derive some satisfaction from affixing blame, but what feels infinitely better is to forgive. Underscore this opportunity in the apologies you make.

Underscore this opportunity, but whatever you do, don't tell your boss (or anyone else) how she should feel. Accidents and errors come in many varieties—this chapter recognizes five —but one basic formula applies to dealing with them all: *Acknowledge the error. Let your boss know that she would be perfectly justified in getting angry. Then thank her for her patient forebearance and understanding. Proceed to positive suggestions for working together to repair any damage.*

When It's Your Fault

What your parents undoubtedly told you is, at least in this case, true. If you screw up, own up.

Generally, you should report the error as soon as possible—since it's better coming from you than if your boss discovers it on her own or some third party makes the revelation. However, do not run into the office in a blaze of guilt-ridden panic. If at all possible, take the time first to assess the nature and degree of the error and, second, to formulate some alternatives for controlling and repairing the damage. Thus armed, report the problem. This does not necessarily mean that you should volunteer your assessment of the degree of damage. Whether or not you do requires careful judgment on your part. Perhaps making an immediate assessment is necessary for the good of a given project or the company in general. On the other hand, if you believe it sufficient to report the particulars of error minimally, all other things being equal, this is probably the better alternative. Why? There is a strategic advantage in giving your boss the feeling that she is assessing the error for herself rather than having to take your "biased" version of it.

If you do feel it necessary to deliver a full report, make every effort to be genuinely objective about it. This cuts two ways. Having made an error, we tend either to move heaven, earth, and the facts in order to excuse and exonerate ourselves, or, at the other extreme, we rush headlong into a *mea culpa* mode, beating our breast and tearing our hair—or the verbal equivalent of these actions. Both extremes are destructive. If you try to minimize an error by worming out of blame, your boss will most likely assume the damage is worse than it is, and you will look like an irresponsible coward. On the other hand, if you launch into an orgy of confession in which you declare yourself the world's worst sinner, the stupidest, most incompetent bonehead ever to walk through corporate doors, she will more than likely believe you. Don't blithely excuse yourself, but don't hand your boss a bullet with your name on it, either. Not only is she likely to use that ammunition, you will also come off looking like an unconfident, self-blaming nebbish.

As a general rule, then, when you make a mistake, pause to assess it, prepare some potential remedies, then report the error as concisely—and as minimally—as the specific circumstance allows. Then follow the procedure outlined above: admit fault; acknowledge your boss's right to be angry; thank her for her patience and understanding; and present whatever alternatives you have in mind.

When It's Not Your Fault

What happens when you encounter an accident or error for which you are not responsible? If it can be done expeditiously, find the person who is responsible and discuss the matter with him as helpfully as possible, always focusing on constructive solutions rather than blame. If it is impossible or impractical to identify the responsible person, and assuming it is a problem you cannot address and solve entirely by yourself or on your own authority, report it to your boss. In doing so, you need to be aware of two harmful tendencies. When we report problems caused by others, we tend to do so either with an exaggerated aura of doom or with a certain irrepressible glee. When you report a problem, you are doing your job. If you allow obnoxious, albeit normal, emotions to intrude, you undo your good work. Remember the nasty habit some ancient rulers had of killing the messenger who brought bad tidings? Don't let this happen to you.

The appropriate alternative is not to ignore problems when you see them ("Don't rock the boat"), but to try to discover the opportunity within the problem. Do you want your boss to perceive you as a problem-solver? Well, first you need a problem. Find one, report it, and suggest solutions.

When It's Not Your Fault But It IS Your Problem

Historians still debate whether World War II General Tomoyuki Yamashita should have been executed as a war criminal for the brutal excesses committed by his subordinates during Japan's last-ditch defense of Manila. After all, he didn't directly order the many atrocities his officers and men committed. But a military tribunal ruled that a commander is, by the very nature of command, ultimately responsible for the actions of subordinates. And Yamashita, accordingly, was hanged.

Depending on who you're working for, you may or may not feel the kind of pressure to which Yamashita was subjected. Unfortunately, however, business presents many situations less extreme but in other ways quite analogous to that of the Japanese general. Your "subordinates" commit any number of atrocities for which you are not directly responsible, but that are, nevertheless, your problem.

If you can handle such problems immediately, efficiently, and effectively without resorting to higher authority, by all means do so. Reporting such errors and accidents can be a delicate and tricky matter. When you must make a report, communicate above all your belief in Harry Truman's universally respected motto: The buck stops here. You may assess fault—your subordinate failed to do something, a supplier failed to deliver, and so on—but you must demonstrate your willingness to take ultimate responsibility. Don't, of course, stop with this and an apology. Turn the event into something positive with a strong response that tells your boss that you are a problem solver.

When You Can't Explain

It would be great if mistakes were never made and accidents never happened. Failing this, it would still be nice if mistakes and accidents could always be explained in the neat, forthright way suggested above. Unfortunately, sometimes things go wrong for, as far as you can tell, no particular reason at all. There are times when you must report an accident or error, but you can't explain it. It is bad enough to have to live with the consequences of a problem, but the occasion when you cannot get a handle on the crisis, cannot instantly demonstrate mastery of the situation, is truly frightening. At a time like this, you need an ally.

You need your boss.

This does not mean that you should go running to him in panic and helplessness. But, if you are genuinely at a loss, the best strategy is to admit it—calmly. "I need your help" is a powerful phrase, practically a magic formula, which even the hardest-hearted boss will find difficult to resist. "I need your help. We are missing three customer files. I don't know why, and I don't know where they could be. Rather than waste more time hunting for them, I'd like to call the clients. How do I do it without embarrassing us?"

Don't dump the problem in your boss's lap, but do enlist his aid.

Suggest as much of a course of action as you can, then don't try to go it alone. Verbally transform the situation from "I" to "we."

When a Project Fails

Thus far, we have been dealing with mistakes, errors, and glitches. But what do you do when you have responsibility for a project that, through no one's particular fault, fails? A product line you've developed doesn't sell, a client you've courted doesn't buy, a contract you've angled for goes to someone else. In cases like this, depending on your employer and your track record, your job may or may not be on the line. Your ego, however, *certainly* is. And it is very hard to communicate strongly and positively when you are feeling bad about yourself.

Yet it is essential that you salvage whatever you can from the wreckage—and much that you salvage can be quite valuable. Those hoary adages from childhood return to us at moments like this, and the hoariest of them all is also the truest: Learn from your mistakes.

It's a fact. The most valuable item of salvage is experience, knowledge. Thomas Edison was weary after thousands of substances he tested as electric light bulb filaments had failed. When someone offered condolences for the waste of so much time and effort, the inventor brushed the well-meaning words aside. We haven't failed, he declared. Now we know thousands of things that will not work as filaments.

In mining knowledge from the ashes of your defeat, you salvage the future. And it is with the future that you must verbally arm yourself when you confront your boss in the wake of failure. Above all, avoid such phrases as "should have," "wish I had," "if I had only," and so on. Substitute instead, "next time," "in the future," "we"—not "I"—"we learned a lesson for the future," "we won't do it this way next time," and so on. Accept responsibility for the present as you must, but hold on to the future, which is, after all, hope, potential, and opportunity.

Words to Use

advice	*control*
advise	*cope*
again	*determine*
apologize	*discuss*
assist	*expedite*
command	*experience*
consider	*formulate*

future
glitch
help
invest
lead
learn
lesson
manage
navigate
plan

reconsider
recoup
recover
regroup
repair
rescue
responsibility
rethink
revise
sorry

Phrases to Use

bear with me
cope with this
damage control
dust ourselves off
emergency measures
for the future
give thought to
I'm sorry
I need your help
in the future
learned a lesson

learned a valuable lesson
make all the necessary
    apologies
make necessary adjustments
minimize damage
next time
pick ourselves up
revise our methods
under control
won't do it that way again

Words to Avoid

blame
catastrophe
crisis
destroyed
disaster
exploded

fault
foul-up
hopeless
mess
misjudged
snafu

Phrases to Avoid

beyond repair
big mistake
bit the big one
blew it
bombed out
can't be fixed
don't blame me
fatal error

huge problem
I can't do anything about it
not my fault
not my problem
screw up
struck out
unavoidable error

Your Script

1.

I made a mistake in the report I submitted to Belcher and Son. The figures for items six and seven are wrong. I tried to catch the documents before they went out of here, but I was too late. I've prepared a corrected report with a cover letter, which I'd like you to read. Assuming you approve, I'll send this to the Belchers by messenger—and I'll call them to tell them it's coming. In the future, I see, we're just going to have to build in a full day's proofreading and fact-checking time.

This is an example of a forthright approach. The speaker admits the error, neither excusing nor judging herself but focusing on the problem and the proposed fix for it. She ends not with regret or self-castigation but with a look toward the future.

2.

The figures are in on the Gas Works promotion. I'd be lying if I said I wasn't very disappointed in the performance of what I thought would be a natural sell. You know, we worked very hard on this, and it's rough on us all when things don't turn out as we had hoped and expected. I'd like to schedule a meeting with you to review the project and see what we can learn from it. I don't want to be disappointed the next time we promote a Gas Works product.

Again, no sugar coating. Without wailing, the speaker lets his boss know that the project did not fail for lack of caring and commitment. He also makes it clear that, far from wanting to run away from the failure, he wants to learn and—in this way, at least—profit from it.

Responses to Anticipate

Don't be too hard on yourself.
Reply with:

☑ *Thanks. I appreciate that. I have no intention of being hard on myself. That's not going to keep this kind of thing from happening again. I do, however, want to take a good, hard look at the problem, analyze it, learn from it, and then discuss it with you.*

Frankly, you're not being hard enough on yourself.
Reply with:

☑ *I take full responsibility for what happened. If I thought an elaborate demonstration of repentance would do anything for our bottom line, I'd be in here with a cat-o'-nine-tails. What I can promise you is that I will be very hard on the causes of the error, and I will not let it happen again.*

Situation 11
The Raise: Handling *No*

The most difficult times to speak up are those situations in which you are made to feel like a child confronted by an authority figure who takes on the form of a parent. In Situations 9 and 10, "Taking Your Lumps" and "Accidents and Errors," we are almost invariably vulnerable to this dynamic. But it is in the present situation—when our boss tells us *no*—that the child-parent relationship comes most powerfully and debilitatingly to the fore.

This happens even to the most grown-up and sophisticated of us. An authority figure issues a negative, and it is like a cold dunk in the Fountain of Youth. The years fall away, and we become children. For some of us, this means sinking into tongue-tied, embarrassed submission. Experiencing *no* summons up images of instant deflation: "He burst my balloon." "She took the wind out of my sails."

For others of us, the childlike response to *no* is a tantrum— either marginally verbal, involving expletives and name-calling, or wholly non-verbal. In an office where I once worked, an irate credit manager put his foot clear through a drywall partition, and a frustrated sales director pulled his phone out by the roots and smashed it to the ground, leaving the heap of electronic guts on the coffee table in his outer office as (I suppose) a kind of trophy or a warning to others.

Deflation, of course, is neither an effective nor satisfying response to *no*, and while both the marginally verbal and the wholly non-verbal responses are dramatic enough to guarantee an effect, it is unlikely that the effect will be the one you want.

Is the answer self-control? That's *an* answer, but a hollow one— like telling yourself not to have feelings. The more effective alternative to simply yielding to the child within you is not attempting *self*-control, but gaining control of the *situation*. Fortunately, regardless of your feelings, it is possible to use words to manage the dynamic between you and your boss. This does not mean that your childlike feelings will disappear. Nor does it guarantee that your boss will change that *no* to *yes*. Effective verbal management of a situation does give you a shot at converting negative to positive, but that's not its primary goal. Your principal object should be not to convert that *no* into a *yes*, but to transform it from a potential disaster, which might damage your relationship with your boss, to an occasion that builds your relationship.

How you handle *no* reveals whatever you want it to reveal about your character and whatever you want it to reveal about your feelings toward your boss. How you handle *no* will teach your boss about *you*. And it is up to you to fashion the appropriate lesson.

If it is more blessed to give than to receive, it is far, far easier to give than to deny. Let's face it. Being turned down for a raise makes you feel terrible, not just simply bad, but bad in a number of confusing ways that come at you all at once. You feel cheated. You feel angry. You feel unappreciated. You feel insecure. You feel inadequate. You feel demoralized. You feel like quitting. You feel like running to someone who *will* appreciate you. You feel like you will never get another job. You feel like your boss is an ingrate and a jerk. You feel like your boss may be right. You feel incompetent. Depending on your financial circumstances, you feel in some degree desperate. And, finally, you feel like an unwanted child.

Now that your feelings are out in the open, what about your boss? How does *she* feel?

Who cares? You should. I'm not going to tell you that, in turning you down for a raise, your boss feels "just as bad" as you do. No. You do, indeed, feel much worse than she does. However, it *is* difficult for most bosses to turn down a request for a raise. Most of us, bosses included—and even those who suffer from a tendency to tyranny, guilt-mongering, anger, and the rest—most of us would rather be liked than disliked. Most of us also realize that people who give you what you want are liked, while those who say *no* are disliked. When your boss says *no* to a raise, then, you are faced with achieving a rather complex goal:

- You want to create the conditions that make it possible for her to give you the raise, if not now, as soon as possible; if not as much as you asked for, as much as possible.

- You want to demonstrate that the *no* has not reduced your commitment to your company or to your boss but, on the contrary, has strengthened your resolve to make the company stronger so that, next time, your boss can say *yes*.

- You want to minimize your boss's bad feelings—not, in truth, to help *her* out, but in the realization that her bad feelings will ultimately influence her relationship with you.

- While you take the *no* in good grace, you do *not* want to communicate acquiescence. This, after all, is yet another of the many negotiations that make up your relationship with your boss. Negotiation should not necessitate one side simply caving in. Both sides should gain something. Keep the negotiation open.

Words to Use

achieve	*negotiate*
achievement	*performance*
appropriate	*plan*
circumstances	*possible*
commitment	*proposal*
conditions	*propose*
consider	*reconsider*
continue	*renegotiate*
feasible	*review*
future	*role*
idea	*service*
instrumental	*understand*
merit	

Phrases to Use

another review	*level of compensation*
at an appropriate time	*make it possible*
at present	*reach an appropriate figure*
by [date]	*review the request again*
in a position to	*work out a schedule*
in the future	*work out a timetable*
I understand	*work toward*

Words to Avoid

angry	*ridiculous*
exploited	*slave*
insist	*unfair*
quit	

Phrases to Avoid

can't be helped	*if . . . then*
given everything to	*if you can't, you can't*
if I don't get a raise, I'll quit	*I have no choice*
if that's the way it is, there's	*inadequate wage*
nothing I can do	*I need this*

it doesn't matter
makes me angry
no two ways
okay
slave wages
that's the way it is, I guess

this leaves me no alternative
we're both powerless
worked my heart out
you give me no choice
you have no choice
you must

Your Script

1.

Of course I'm disappointed that the company is not in a position to raise my salary at this time. Can we sit down now and talk about a compromise figure?

2.

Of course I'm disappointed that the company is not in a position to raise my salary at this time. I'd like to set up a firm date for review of the situation. When would it be possible to review my request again?

3.

I know it's difficult for you to turn me down. It's hard to be turned down, too. So, can we discuss what it will take for me to help us get into a position where you do not have to turn me down?

4.

I understand that there are pressures operating on the company, and you know that I'm committed to making as much money for the company as possible. I have gone more than fourteen months without a salary increase, however. Can we set a date for another review? I suggest some point within ninety days as an appropriate time.

5.

It would help me very much if you could detail your reasons for turning down my request and, more important, let me know what would make it possible for you to say "yes" three months from now.

All of these responses are intended to keep the door open. They are also aimed at securing *something*—if not the raise, at least a date when the matter can be brought up for reconsideration. Perhaps none of these approaches seems sufficiently hard-nosed. You don't need this book to tell you how to make threats. That you can do on your own. But threats are seldom productive of anything except hostility. If you are poorly compensated and repeatedly turned down for salary increases, it is not time to threaten your employer, it is time to look for a new job. The approaches suggested here assume that you want to remain with your current company and grow within it. Besides, do bear in mind that any request for a salary increase—even the most reasonably and politely framed—is, in and of itself, a threat. It communicates to your boss that you are not entirely satisfied and that, while you promise to remain loyal and productive, well, you *will* be receptive to offers from elsewhere.

Responses to Anticipate

This is a bad time to ask. I'd have to say no.
Reply with:

☑ *I certainly don't want to continue the discussion at a time when you have to say "no." When would be a more appropriate time to review my request?*

I can't promise that I'll be in any better position three months from now.
Reply with:

☑ *I'm not looking for promises. I am asking if it is possible, appropriate, and reasonable to make this request again in ninety days.*

I don't see the possibility of a raise for quite some time.
Reply with:

☑ *You know that, as long as I am working here, I will give you 100 percent. I am, of course, eager to be compensated at an appropriate level. I would appreciate your reviewing the situation and giving me a firm date for us to have another conversation.*

Situations 12 and 13
The Final Frontier

If it's all over, why keep talking?

Quitting or getting fired does not mean it's all over. Unless things have gone very badly indeed, the fact that your employment has been terminated does not mean you and your boss have been wiped from the face of the earth. Depending on what you do for a living, the business world can be quite small, and, whether you're leaving a job voluntarily or not, it is quite possible that you and your boss will cross paths again. You may even return to the firm. Termination can be a positive event; don't let your words make it negative. But even when termination is nasty and unwanted, don't turn a bad thing into something worse.

Quitting and getting fired are final—but only relatively so. What you say can help determine the degree of finality. Use words to keep your termination as open-ended as possible.

QUITTING

Let's pause a minute before we send you on your way. Usually one quits a job only after securing some other means of livelihood. Either you make a decision to go into business for yourself, or you've found another job. Before you announce your resignation, *think*. Do you absolutely want to quit? Or do you want to use the job offer you've just gotten as a bargaining chip with your present company?

Unless you are firmly bent on leaving, you should approach the "terminal" conversation *as if* you are willing to entertain (or are even seeking) a counteroffer from your boss. Instead, then, of beginning with something like, "I have accepted an offer from . . .," start with "I have received an offer from." Give the particulars, including money and other conditions that make the offer attractive. As you know by now, I am all in favor of doing whatever is necessary—verbally—to give your boss the feelings you want him to have. However, you should not lie about a job offer. Your boss may just call your bluff or, in the small world of business, he may well check out your story and catch you in that lie. A job offer is, indeed, a great bargaining tool. Just make sure you really do have the offer before you introduce it into the conversation.

Even if you are certain that you don't want to use the offer as leverage in your present position, that all you want is *out*, you should still be in no hurry to slam the verbal doors behind you. You quit a job for a wide variety of reasons: a better job comes along; you hate your present job; you hate your boss; you don't get paid enough; you're bored. Whatever. In general, regardless of your reasons for leaving and your feelings about the job and the boss you are leaving, your "terminal" conversation should be framed as positively as possible—in a way that puts your soon-to-be-former boss, his company, and yourself in the best possible light. This does not mean that you should lie—"I love this job, and it just kills me to quit"—but it does mean that you should avoid concentrating on the negative reasons that have motivated your decision and emphasize the positive instead. Rather than tell your boss something like, "I'm quitting because there is no opportunity in this dead-end job," you might put it this way: "I've decided to accept a position that offers me the kind of opportunities for advancement that, at least for now, we can't match here." The message in both statements is that you need room for growth. The first statement makes this declaration and then, quite rudely, slams the door in the listener's face. The second statement pulls no punches; you are leaving because you have found a position that promises more than your present job can offer. Yet you have left the door ever-so-slightly ajar: "at least for now." Even more important, although you are, indeed, leaving, you are not *running for your life*. That "we" is a carefully chosen and very effective word.

Why bother with all this? What if you never, ever intend to work for this guy again? What if, in fact, he's been a real jerk, and you are weeping with gratitude to be getting away?

The object is not to soften the blow of your departure, or even to make your boss feel good. The object is to demonstrate that you are a valuable person, a business asset, and that you are fully aware of your value. Verbally charging out of the office and slamming the door is not the behavior of a self-confident person in control of his present actions and his likely future. Leaving the office—again, I am speaking about your verbal management of the situation—leaving the office gracefully and graciously, with honesty tempered by courtesy, dramatically demonstrates the image you have of yourself. There is a difference between *quitting*—a word that connotes exhaustion, desperation, despair, and even deficiency of character—and *moving on to something better* (or *new*, or *different*).

If you plan your departure carefully, you can also offer your boss something more than good words. Make it clear that you will do everything possible to ease the transition for your replacement. This, of course, is a promise you can make only if you have given sufficient notice of your departure. It pays to allow for this in your plans, however, since engineering a smooth transition will go a long way toward defusing any smoldering resentment.

Everything I've said assumes that you are leaving under no extraordinary duress. There are, of course, work situations that are manifestly intolerable. In the most extreme instances—where you have been subjected to sexual, racial, or other harassment, for example—you may want not only to leave but to seek legal advice and assistance. Short of this, in situations where you simply cannot stand the job, you may find it inappropriate or even impossible to stress anything positive. In such cases, you may want to speak frankly with your boss, listing your grievances in as emotionally neutral a manner as possible. Usually, however, the better strategy is to put it into writing, always keeping the discourse at a factual rather than an emotional level.

Words to Use

career	*memories*
continue	*new*
contributed	*opportunity*
different	*our*
enjoyed	*pleasant*
family	*regret*
future	*rewarding*
grateful	*satisfying*
help	*start*
helpful	*transition*
learned	*us*
loyal	*we*

Phrases to Use

break new ground	*move on*
delightful memories	*next step in my career*
difficult for me to do this	*opportunity for development*
feel like one of the family	*personal fulfillment*
keep in touch	*seize a new opportunity*
leave with some regret	*something I need to do*
level of compensation	*will never forget*
mixed emotions	*will always remember*
more room to maneuver	*wonderful experience*

Words to Avoid

bad	*dumb*
better	*quit*
bored	*stuck*
cheap	*tedious*
confining	*unappreciated*
dull	

Phrases to Avoid

bad pay	*just one of those things*
can do better than this	*low wages*
dead-end job	*no future*
I'm fed up	*no opportunity*
I've had it	*you don't appreciate me*
just can't seem to get along	

Your Script

1.

This is the hardest thing I've ever had to say to you, so I better just come out and say it. I've been offered a position as senior analyst with Chase & Fly at a salary of $55,000. As you know, that's more than we're in a position to ante up here. Add to that the way management is structured over there—well, I've got a faster track to account executive than what might be offered here. This place has been like family to me, but for the sake of my career, I don't see how I can turn down the offer.

This opening reflects a sincere intention to leave the company, coupled with equally sincere regrets about doing so, while leaving the door ajar for a counteroffer.

2.

I've been approached by Felton Felt Products with an offer of a position as assistant sales manager. I haven't said "yes" yet, but I've got to tell you that it is a very attractive offer to me—despite the loyalty I feel to our company and to you personally. The salary is 25 percent higher, and the opportunities for advancement seem considerably greater. They want me to start in four weeks.

This one's a harder sell, leaving the door open even wider. The message is that you are prepared to accept the offer, but you are also very receptive to a counteroffer.

3

I've worked here six years, and during that time I've gotten very close to a lot of people, including you. That's why it's not easy for me to tell you that I am accepting an offer from Benjamin Franklin Printing Company as a press manager. The money, the hours, and the job security are just too inviting to pass up. Even with all that, it's a hard decision. I've learned a lot here, but it is time to move on to a position of broader responsibility.

This is about as firmly as you should close the door behind you. Unless your boss is very devoted to you, this "terminal" announcement does not invite a counteroffer. Even so, the speaker deliberately avoids absolute finality by saying that she "is accepting" rather than "has accepted."

Responses to Anticipate

What would it take to make you change your mind?
Reply with:

☑ *I'll admit it. I would love it if you could make it impossible for me to take the offer. [Then go on to list what you want: salary, hours, vacation, working conditions, position, etc.] That's what I would need to turn down the offer in good conscience.*

You can't leave at a time like this.
Reply with:

☑ *I know this isn't the best time for you. But it is when the offer came. For me, it is a case of act now or miss the opportunity— and this is an opportunity I literally cannot afford to miss. I've got three weeks. You have my assurance that I'll do whatever is necessary to ease the transition for you.*

I feel betrayed.
Reply with:

☑ *Please. You must know that my leaving has nothing to do with you or with the company. It's a matter of opportunity for me. I don't see this as leaving Smith and Son, but as doing what is necessary to build my career. If I could do it as effectively by staying, I would. It is very hard for me to leave.*

I've enjoyed working with you, and I wish you the best of luck.
Reply with:

☑ *Thanks. Coming from you, well, that means a very great deal to me. I know that we'll be staying in touch, and I am grateful to you for having made this a rewarding experience.*

GETTING FIRED

Don't let anybody tell you that getting fired is not the end of the world. At the moment it comes, it might as well be.

You are assailed by terrible emotions: a sense of failure and embarrassment coupled with a fear of losing your house, your car—of being unable to provide for your family. You may feel that you will never get another job or that, having gotten one, you can never regain your old confidence.

Volumes have been written on what to do if you get fired. I can offer only two pieces of advice on what to do (I'll have more to offer on what to *say*):

- Get another job.

- Be aware, while you are in the process of getting another job, that thousands of people are fired each and every day. They feel much as you do. Then they go out and get another job.

The end of the world? It certainly feels like it. And it can be genuinely disastrous. Sometimes.

Rarely, actually. Nasty as it is, getting fired is in fact a normal (not inevitable, but normal) phase of the employment cycle. It happens. It is far from desirable, but it is also far from exceptional. Chances are very good that you will survive. You might even get a better job.

When you are overwhelmed with anger and fear, it is very difficult to practice effective verbal management. Yet it is crucial at this point. As it is best to leave the door ajar—however slightly—when you voluntarily leave a job, so it is best to make it possible for your boss to leave the door open a crack when he hands you your walking papers. This may be difficult or impossible to do if you are being dismissed "for cause"—failure to do your assigned job, misconduct, excessive absenteeism, poor performance, etc. But as is more often the case, if you are being laid off because of economic conditions, corporate reorganization, or phase-out of a program, it is vital to keep all hope alive. Yes, you *will* get yourself another job, but do what you can to make it possible for you to return to *this* one.

Dismissal for cause does not usually come out of the blue. It generally follows warnings and employee conferences. If you feel that you are being treated unjustly, plan to seek counsel from the appropriate union, or professional or governmental agency. You may want to secure legal advice as well. For the moment—the moment of dismissal—it is generally best to threaten nothing. Do, however, make clear your position that you are being treated unfairly, that you have endeavored to perform well for the company, and that you feel you deserve better treatment. You might ask, quite straightforwardly, if there is an alternative course open: temporary separation during a review process, for example.

In cases where the dismissal is made without prejudice, perhaps even with regret, because of economic or other circumstances, you should respond by letting your boss know that, while he has fired you, you have not dismissed him. You are greatly dismayed by the news, of course, since you have found working here such a rewarding experience. Determine, in conversation with your boss, whether the dismissal is permanent or temporary. Might you expect to be hired in another capacity at another time? What circumstances would make continuation of this position—or hiring in another position—possible? By no means should you desperately beg for your job, but do let your boss know that you retain a commitment to the company.

Words to Use

alternatives	reconsider
appropriate	record
circumstances	reevaluate
commitment	regret
delay	responsible
discuss	review
extend	rewarding
fairness	service
hope	shocked
negotiate	strategy
possibility	stunned
possible	suspend
propose	temporary

Phrases to Use

arrive at a strategy	make it possible to
explore alternatives	responsible alternatives
explore appropriate	What are the alternatives?
alternatives	What would make it
Is there any possibility?	possible . . .

Words to Avoid

all expletives	hopeless
destroyed	outraged
devastated	ruined

Phrases to Avoid

all threats	who needs it
good riddance	why me?
how can you do this?	you can't do this
I can get a better job on a	you can't fire me
moment's notice	you can't fire me, I quit!
I didn't like this job anyway	you haven't heard the end
I'm going to sue	of this
I won't let this happen	you'll hear from my lawyer

Your Script

1.

Boss: *I'm afraid that, due to corporate restructuring, we're going to have to let you go, effective two weeks from today. I wish there were something I could do about it.*

You: *I don't have to tell you, this is a shock. Let me digest this news for a day or two, and then I'd like to discuss the situation with you.*

Since you have some time, the best thing to do is delay your response, rather than stammer something while you are under the most pressure. When you return later for a conversation, raise the possibility of alternatives to dismissal, discuss the permanence of the dismissal (Is there a chance of rehiring and, if so, when?), and go over with your boss ways in which he is willing to help you find another job.

2.

Boss: *As you know, we have not been satisfied with your performance. I'm afraid at this point I have no choice but to let you go. The severance is effective immediately. I've prepared a severance check for you.*

You: *I would be lying if I told you this is entirely unexpected. I had hoped, however, that we could work out some alternative to dismissal. I've enjoyed working here, and I believe I've given this company a lot. Since your decision does seem final, I'll leave without further discussion—except to tell you that I honestly believe you are losing an able, skilled, and loyal employee.*

There is no room to maneuver here. Leave with dignity, including a statement meant to set the record straight.

3.

Boss: *It's clear we're not getting along together. I've decided to terminate our working relationship, effective two weeks from today.*

You: *I am sorry you feel this way and, of course, even sorrier that you feel you must take such an extreme action. Since your decision seems to be based on feeling, it would help me very much if we could talk again before I leave. It would also be very helpful—and, I think, appropriate—if you could put your reasons for my dismissal more concretely and specifically, perhaps in the form of a letter. I have enjoyed working here, and I sincerely believe that I am good for this company. I don't want to leave without knowing exactly what went wrong.*

This accomplishes three things. It leaves the door slightly ajar. It does not let your boss off the hook so easily, but compels him to review his decision. And it underscores your commitment to the firm.

Responses to Anticipate

We have nothing further to discuss.

Reply with:

☑ *I don't agree. Other than knowing that you are somehow dissatisfied with my performance, I've very little idea of why I'm being fired. That is what we have to discuss, and I would like to discuss it.*

I can't hold out much hope for another job here soon.

Reply with:

☑ *I'm not asking for much hope. I want to leave here with good feelings on all sides, and I want you to know that, no matter where I go from here, I'm always eager to hear of opportunities at Rackem and Sons.*

The matter is closed.

Reply with:

☑ *For you it may be, but I have a lot of questions without answers. I would like to ask them, and I would like to hear the answers. I don't intend to argue. I just want to find out what went wrong.*

Part Three

And Everyone Else

The Accountant

I used to think that most people are intimidated by money. I was wrong. What actually intimidates most of us is the feeling that we are not in *control* of our money. This is not a neurotic fear but a healthy and realistic one. In a complex society, money is, after all, life's blood. Our survival depends on it. Yet it is also true, in a complex society, that all too often we trust the manipulation of this precious commodity to others. The tax code of the United States is Byzantine in its complexity, and many of us, perfectly competent when it comes to *making* money, dissolve into a quivering mass of gelatin when it comes to figuring out what portion of our take belongs to Uncle Sam and the myriad other jurisdictions to which we may be subject. Quite rightly, we hire an accountant to advise us or even to make these determinations for us. With the possible exception of a physician, there is no other hired professional to whom we entrust so much of our lives. Obviously, such a sensitive relationship demands a high degree of effective communication. Unfortunately, in this relationship communication is often slighted or virtually dispensed with altogether.

Part of this is due to the seasonal nature of an accountant's work. We customarily load her down in the weeks preceding April 15. She barely has time to hit all the right calculator keys, let alone talk to all of her clients. Part of the lack of communication is due to a conviction that numbers speak louder than words. Give me the right figures, the accountant says, and we don't need to talk.

But the communication gap has two sides. Most of us are reluctant to talk about the money we make. Most of us feel that we don't make enough, for one thing, and suffer a certain nagging shame about our meager hoard. There is also ingrained in us from childhood a sense that money is unclean. We are taught to dig into our wallets furtively. We are taught that coin of the realm is "filthy lucre." Sure, nobody really *thinks* this. But the feeling is there—a trace of it—nonetheless. The point is that a number of factors discourage us from effectively communicating with our accountant. Our impulse is to hand her a shoebox full of receipts and forms and let her worry about it all. Take it off my hands. It'll all come out all right. After all, it's only—blood.

The first step toward establishing effective communications with your accountant is to manage your financial life to allow plenty of time to talk. For most of us, this boils down to having your income tax materials prepared as close to the first of the year as possible. April 1 is way too late, and March is pushing it. The next step is to realize something about accountants as a group. Like dentists, they tend to be well paid, and also like dentists, they tend to suffer from vocational image problems. For most of us, arithmetic is boring; therefore (we reason) anyone who spends her life adding numbers must also be boring. In the corporate world, accountants are often called bean counters—not raiders, or sharks, or hatchet men, or whiz kids, or managers, or account executives, but bean counters. That's got to do something to a person's professional ego.

I'm not making this observation in order to cut the intimidating accountant down to size, but to suggest that a good way to establish effective communications with her is to demonstrate that, far from dismissing her as a mere bean counter, you regard your accountant as a valued counselor, advisor, and strategist. Give her these feelings, and you are bound to get her ear and her brains.

You would not expect your accountant to work in the absence of the appropriate figures—income, outgo, losses, and so on. Neither should you expect to talk to your accountant meaningfully without arming yourself with a list of the issues you wish to address. Prepare for the conversation by listing financial goals and concerns. Before you embark on the conversation, decide what you want to accomplish by means of the conversation. Then stick to your agenda.

Words to Use

advantageous	*appreciate*
advice	*appropriate*
aggressively	*assurance*
alternative	*confidence*
analysis	*counsel*

downside
expedite
experience
grateful
informed
judgment
opinion
options
positive
reliance

rely
responsible
risk
safety
security
thanks
trust
upside
value
wisdom

Phrases to Use

advise me on
best-case scenario
call on your experience
call on your expertise
conservative course
educated guess
explore the alternatives

informed opinion
in your experience
I trust you on this
solid advice
what would you do?
worst-case scenario

Words to Avoid

ballpark
irresponsible
outrageous

sharp
waste

Phrases to Avoid

cut corners
fake it
*how hard can it be to add
    and subtract*
how long can it take
I leave it entirely up to you

it's about time
just give me your best guess
take the shortest route
you're calling the shots
you're the boss

Your Script

1.

I'm working on a tight budget, and I can't be as conservative as I might like to be. I'm willing to live with a certain amount of risk. I'd like you to go after deductions aggressively, but in cases where you have any doubt at all, I would really appreciate your careful counsel. I've turned in my numbers to you early because I'd like to get a handle on my taxes as early as possible, and before I make any decisions, I'd like us to have some time to sit down and discuss strategy—before you are caught in the tax-season crunch.

Explain clearly what you want. Provide guidelines, but don't dictate. Establish a speaking relationship early.

2.

You: *It's getting close to April 15, and I'm beginning to feel uncomfortable. I want to have time to review my return with you.*

Accountant: *Just leave it to me. Don't worry. I'll do it right.*

You: *I'm not afraid that you'll make mistakes. But I do want to review the return with you—at some leisure—to make sure that you and I are agreed on the goals we're trying to reach here.*

Make it clear that you value the accountant as a professional, but that you are not passively handing your life over to her. As with many effective verbal strategies, the object here is to create a team.

Responses to Anticipate

Don't you trust me?

Reply with:

☑ *Of course I trust you. That's why we're working together. But I am a hands-on person. I am not comfortable turning over any aspect of my business to anyone—no matter how much I trust them. I want to work on this together. So, please, let's make the time.*

I can't be doing a lot of second-guessing.

Reply with:

☑ *That's just why I want to sit down over this now. I want all the advice you can give me, and I want a return we can both be pleased with.*

Your work is in process. Don't worry.

Reply with:

☑ *Great! Let's monitor the process soon, then. Is early next week good for you?*

The Appliance Repairperson

The good news here is that most people who come out to your home to fix something that doesn't work are strongly motivated to make things right. It feels good to do a job well and to bask in the gratitude of the homemaker whose $900 refrigerator just quit with two weeks' worth of food in jeopardy. It is also a fact that, most of the time, little communication between you and the repairperson is necessary—beyond a clear, concise explanation of the problem.

There is still plenty of room for minor disasters, however. While the repairperson may be eager to perform well once he is at your house, getting him there when you want him can be difficult.

Then what happens if things don't go right the first time, when you are dissatisfied with the repair and must call the repairperson again?

Appliance repair is a business, whether the technician is independent or works for the manufacturer, and recalls are not profitable. It is not impossible that the repairperson will try to convince you that there is nothing wrong with the appliance he just fixed.

First, the matter of securing timely service. You must assume that just about everyone who calls for a repair cries *emergency*. Doubtless, many such calls *are* emergencies—though hardly life-threatening. Clothes can't get washed, food spoils, the television is down and your four-year-old is getting pretty ugly. It is best not to cry wolf but to be emphatic about just what the problem and its consequences are. "The clothes are piling up here. I've got a full-time job and can't get to the laundromat. Can you send somebody over right away?" Or: "I've got hundreds of dollars' worth of food that's going to go bad. I'd run over to my neighbor's with it, but she won't be back until this evening. Can you get somebody over here fast and help me out?" Make the nature of your problem specific, and the person on the other end of the phone will visualize your predicament. The natural impulse under such circumstances is to help.

Once you have the repairman at your house, carefully explain the problem—even if he has it written up as a result of your phone call. Tell him what you want done—if it is something more than the obvious task of simply getting the appliance to work. "Now it's stopped working altogether, but even when it was working, the thermostat never operated properly. Please take a look at that as well and tell me what you need to do to get it fixed." Before the repairperson leaves, ask him what, exactly, had gone wrong and what you can do to prevent it in the future. Also, most importantly, make sure that the appliance now works to your satisfaction. If it does not, tell the repairperson before he leaves. In most cases, he will want you to be satisfied and will do whatever is necessary. But you cannot take this for granted. Sticking your head in dishwashers all day can tempt anyone to deny problems. Do not accuse the repairperson of any negligence or wrongdoing. Just attempt to focus him on the appliance and the problem:

> *"That noise wasn't there before. It's unusual."*
>
> *"No, it's perfectly normal."*
>
> *"It's not something I've heard before, and as long as the machine sounds like that, I can't consider it repaired. I need you to take care of that."*

No accusations. Just be insistent about what you require. The object here is not to be *right* or to get your way or to bully the repairperson. The object is to get the appliance working to your satisfaction.

If a repair goes bad and it is necessary to recall the repairperson, it is best to do so without anger or irritation. However, you should—in objective, factual terms—underscore the inconvenience you are suffering. "The refrigerator went out again. Same problem; it just stopped working. I had to stay home three hours Monday waiting for the repairperson. This is really messing up my schedule. Can you get somebody here within the hour?"

When the repair is performed successfully, don't forget to thank the technician. He will appreciate it.

Words to Use

abnormal	*inoperative*
cost	*malfunction*
defective	*normal*
delay	*pleased*
difficult	*problem*
expedite	*satisfaction*
failed	*schedule*
fast	*service*
happy	*thanks*
help	*timely*
inconvenience	*unhappy*
incorrect	*wrong*

Phrases to Use

appreciate your expediting the repair	*losing money*
backed into a corner	*losing time*
disgusted with the machine	*not happy with*
grateful for	*not satisfied with*
greatly appreciate	*piling up*
help me as fast as possible	*problem on my hands*
help me out	*send somebody as soon as you can*
in a jam	*take another look at*

Words to Avoid

*emergency (unless it really   lazy
     is)   slow*
incompetent

Phrases to Avoid

*bad job   send me somebody who
can't get away with that   knows what they're
do it right this time   doing
get it right now   you and I both know
I'll speak to your manager*

Your Script

1.

My washing machine broke down. I've got a full-time job that leaves me no time to get to a laundromat on short notice, and, let me tell you, with three children, it doesn't take long for the clothes to pile up. Please, please, please send me someone fast.

Humanize your call for help with some vivid detail that paints a picture of your predicament.

2.

You: *I hear a grinding noise. That's not something I can live with. Please check it out again.*

Repairperson: *I don't hear anything.*

You: *Well, I've lived with the machine for three years now, and I can tell you that it has never sounded like that.*

Repairperson: *Seems normal to me.*

You: *Nevertheless, I'm not satisfied with the repair. I will be satisfied if you get rid of that grinding.*

It can be difficult to be insistent without being obnoxious. The best way is to focus on the repair problem, not on the ego of the repairperson. Not "*You* are an idiot" but "I'm not satisfied with the *repair.*"

3.

The refrigerator you repaired on Monday just quit again. Same problem: it's completely dead. Besides the fact that I've got a lot of food that's going to spoil, I just can't afford to keep missing work. I would be very grateful if you would come over right away and help me out.

Again, this is not the time for accusations. Concentrate on the repair, but make it clear that this second breakdown is causing you significant problems.

Responses to Anticipate

I can't promise that we'll be able to get out to you right away.
Reply with:

☑ *I certainly appreciate the fact that you are busy. But I'm in a jam here myself. I'm on a tight schedule, and I need to get this thing working fast. Let's set something up now.*

Look, I'm the expert, and I'm telling you that there is nothing wrong with the machine.
Reply with:

☑ *I appreciate your expertise, but I can show you that the machine just does not get dishes clean. We've been over the kind of detergent I use and the temperature of the water. The problem isn't there. The problem is that the dishes just aren't getting clean. Until the machine gets them clean, I can't be satisfied with the repair. I'd like you to take another look.*

The Audio/Video/Computer Salesperson

It is not my intention in this book to reinforce your negative feelings about any group or profession by slandering it. Consumer electronics sales personnel are often highly professional and very helpful. Since they deal primarily in high-tech luxury items that give people pleasure, they often enjoy their work, and, as a result, buying that stereo or VCR can be quite a pleasant experience.

What problems there are tend to occur in two areas: technobabble and narrow-margin high pressure.

In plain English, we are afraid of being made to look stupid (and being pegged as a sucker) by our lack of technical knowledge or command of the jargon, and we are wary of being pressured by a salesperson working on commission in a heavily discounted, very competitive marketplace. These feelings can lead us to pass up a perfectly good deal, or to make a perfectly bad deal (spending too much for something we don't really want), or they can turn what should be an enjoyable shopping experience into an event marred by anxiety and racked by self-doubt and second-guessing. Consumer electronics purchases are generally little indulgences we allow ourselves. Bad feelings about buying a new hi-fi VCR reduce the value of this electronic toy at least as much as if a part turned out to be defective.

It is important to prepare yourself to speak up to the salesperson before you enter the store. One aspect of the preparation is more or less technical, and the other is strictly emotional. The fact is that the more you educate yourself about stereos, CD players, VCRs, or computers—whatever piece of hardware you are in the market for—the better your chances of making a *good* deal, the *right* deal, and of being satisfied with your purchase. Spend some time talking to owners of such equipment, peruse relevant consumer electronics magazines, or pick up one of the many inexpensive paperback buying guides. You might want to write down your requirements on a sort of informal spec sheet and take it with you to the store. Another useful strategy is to visit more than one dealer and talk to the salespeople about what you want. The important thing at this stage, however, is to make these visits with the firm intention of concluding no purchase—yet. (Don't tell the salesperson this, however.)

At this point, you are using the salesperson as an information resource. (Don't tell the salesperson this, either.) If you are like most everyone else, the kid-in-a-candy-store syndrome makes it difficult to resist the impulse to plunk down your cash and take home the goodies right away. ("That money is burning a hole in your pocket," my mother used to say to me.) At the very minimum, when it *is* time to make the purchase, you should be armed with a clear idea of *what* you want, if not what exactly to buy. For example, do you want to play your VCR through your stereo system? If so, you probably want to pay extra for hi-fi sound. If not, you'll save money by getting a good mono machine. Do you want to do simple word processing on that personal computer? Or do you intend to run a small business with it, doing word processing, spreadsheets, and databases? Buy accordingly.

The second aspect of preparation is emotional, and it boils down to a single imperative: *When you walk into the store, be prepared to walk out empty-handed.* Let's state this even more succinctly: *Be ready to walk away from any deal.*

The principle is simple, but that candy-store syndrome can make it difficult to stick to. It is hard, after all, to transform an experience of self-indulgence into one of (apparent) self-denial. But unless you are prepared *not* to buy, you are granting the salesperson an inordinate degree of power over you, and having given up so much power, it becomes a formidable task to speak up.

Avoiding a bad deal involves, in part, overriding your emotions, your impulse to indulge yourself quite literally at any cost. This is true generally of the art of "speaking up," which often means speaking *over* or *in spite of* what you may feel at the moment. However, your feelings can also help you, especially when it comes to avoiding a bad deal in a consumer electronics salesroom. If you get a "bad feeling" about the place—if the merchandise doesn't look right or you feel unduly pressured, for example—either get out or proceed with extra caution.

You will also feel more comfortable if you observe the following guidelines:

- Ask about the store's warranty and return policies.
- Pay by check or credit card—even if you are offered a small discount for cash. You can always stop a check or adjust a credit debit, but once cash is in the hands of another, it's gone.

Words to Use

adequate	*investigate*
advise	*need*
ask	*negotiate*
assist	*opinion*
benefit	*optimum*
best	*problems*
choice	*return*
choose	*review*
compare	*service*
evaluate	*specifications*
explain	*think*
guarantee	*trade*
help	*useful*
information	*warranty*
informative	*why*
inquire	

Phrases to Use

Are you sure this is your best price?	*please demonstrate*
comparison shop	*please give me your opinion*
explain it to me	*return policy*
Is this all?	*the best you can do for me*
lay it out for me	*What would you buy?*
look elsewhere	*What would you do?*
	your best price

Words to Avoid

anxious	*now*
browse	*today*
eager	*want*
immediately	

Phrases to Avoid

can't wait	*really want*
how much does it cost?	*right away*
I'll take it	*right now*
just looking	*wrap it up*

Your Script

1.

I'm looking for a good, solid, low-end VCR. I'm not interested in complex programming capability or in hi-fi sound, but I do want something solid and dependable that will take hard use. It's for my son.

Concisely but clearly state what you are looking for. Set a limit on features and extras, but it is usually best not to begin with a money figure.

2.

I've been doing some comparison shopping for a monitor-television. I'm interested in getting the sharpest picture possible on a twenty-seven-inch screen, and I'd like stereo capability. What can you show me, and what can you tell me about what you have?

Here is a good way to get information from a salesperson. It let him know that you are not a mere browser, that you are a careful shopper, and that, while you are seriously in the market for the television, you are not necessarily prepared to pull out your checkbook here and now.

3.

Salesperson: *Of course you'll want an MTS decoder and something with an S-VHS jack.*

You: *It depends what these will add to the price. I have no plans to get an S-VHS machine. Tell me more about the MTS decoder and why I should want it.*

You don't have to look like a dope or an easy mark just because you are not fully familiar with the jargon.

4.

You: *Are you sure $535 is the best price you can give me? Seems on the high side.*

Salesperson: *How much cheaper do you want it?*

You: *Well, of course, I'd like it a lot cheaper. But what I had in mind is not spending more than $450. Where can we meet in between?*

Bargaining is not bullying or demanding but negotiating. Here you have set a reasonable desirable price, but you've indicated a willingness to spend somewhat more. Instead of making a demand, you've made an offer.

5.

Salesperson: *You have to act now, because this is the last one we've got. The warranty is fine. It's not a U.S. warranty, but it's fine. Believe me. If you want to spend $200 more, you can go to a fancier store and get a U.S. warranty. But at this price, I just can't guarantee this unit will be here in another hour, let alone tomorrow.*

You: *I appreciate your time. I need to shop around some more, and I'll just have to take my chances on your selling the TV before I come back. Thanks for the warning.*

This kind of crude pressure is all too common. Don't cave in, and don't get angry. Just get out.

Responses to Anticipate

You won't find a better price anywhere else.
Reply with:

☑ *I hope you're wrong about that, since this is more than I wanted to spend.*

How much do you want to spend?
Reply with:

☑ *I'd prefer to tell you exactly what I'm looking for. Then you tell me what it will cost.*

Don't you trust me?
Reply with:

☑ *I don't know you. I can tell you that you haven't convinced me yet that these features make this unit worth $250 more than the other one.*

The Auto Mechanic

No mere worldly possession creates more anxiety than the automobile. For most of us, a great deal of our freedom, pleasure, even our livelihood depends on our car. Yet, for most of us, a car consumes cash as voraciously as it does gasoline. We pay for the machine itself. We pay for fuel. We pay for insurance, license, parking—and for repair and maintenance. Whenever I've moved to a new town, I've asked friends, neighbors, and colleagues to recommend a good mechanic long before I asked any of them to recommend a good doctor.

The similarity of physician to mechanic is striking. Most of us know as little about the internal workings of our cars as we do about our bodies. When something goes wrong, we trustingly turn both over to an expert. Sometimes I think the only visible difference between a physician and a mechanic is that the one is generally cleaner than the other—though some foreign-import mechanics do wear white lab coats, and I have known one "technician" who wore surgical gloves (the grease irritated his skin, he explained).

Sadly, many of us feel intimidated by physicians and mechanics. They tell us what "needs" to be done, and, with little or no questioning, we pay them to do it. It's not their fault. Most good doctors want to discuss treatment and answer questions, and the same holds true for good mechanics. In fact, speaking up to your mechanic is a litmus test of how good he is. If your questions seem to annoy him or if he is evasive, get your car to another shop. By the same token, if your mechanic is a professional, your questions will alert him to the fact that you are informed and concerned. Far from putting him off, they will probably elicit better performance.

When you bring your car in for servicing or repair, begin by listing whatever problems you are experiencing and tell the mechanic what you expect to be done about them. "The brakes are not performing well, and they also make a grinding noise. I want to get those working 100 percent. The air conditioner is not working very well—just not very cold. It's an old car, and I don't want to put a lot of money into it. Please take a look at the air conditioner and tell me what needs to be done. I'll decide whether or not to proceed with repairs." If you anticipate that the car needs a lot of work, you might ask that the mechanic prioritize the jobs for you, differentiating between what needs to be done now, what can wait, and what is strictly optional.

Establishing clear lines of communication at the outset prevents a lot of problems later. But, of course, you can still run into difficulty, usually in three areas:

- The mechanic fails to have the car ready when promised.
- The actual costs significantly exceed the estimated costs.
- The repair is faulty or doesn't solve the problem.

Delivery time should be set when you bring the car in. Beyond this, make it clear that it is important for the mechanic to deliver when promised. "I need the car for a job tomorrow morning, so I'm really depending on getting it this afternoon." No matter how emphatic you are about timeliness, however, you should telephone well before the deadline to monitor progress. "It *will* be ready at five o'clock, then?" If the answer is "no," make it clear that you were depending on timely delivery. What is the problem? What can be done to expedite the work at this point? If the delay is no great inconvenience to you, you should certainly not manufacture artificial rage. However, you should not simply let the mechanic off the hook. You want to communicate to him that he has made a promise and that, while you understand work often takes longer than anticipated, you had counted on delivery when promised. What is his plan for getting the car to you as soon as possible?

Problems with costs exceeding estimates can be prevented in large measure by monitoring the progress of work before you come to pick up the car. Make sure that the mechanic understands that he is to call you before proceeding if the cost of work will exceed the estimate by, say, 10 percent. Most work orders have a line for specifying that such a call be made. But what if, despite precautions, you are presented with a bill that exceeds the estimate? If—as is almost certainly the case—the estimate is non-binding, you have little legal recourse. Besides, you want to get your car, and the mechanic is not likely to release it until you have paid. This does not mean that you should simply cave in.

No mechanic wants his customers to go away unhappy, and repeat business is far more profitable than deliberately overcharging on a single occasion, losing the customer, and (before long) acquiring a bad reputation. We fail to communicate effectively when we feel powerless, when it seems like the other guy holds all the cards. This may appear to be one of those occasions, but think your way through it. The mechanic has failed to please you, and therefore his continued business with you is in jeopardy. It behooves you to exploit the situation. Begin by asking for an explanation of why the estimate and the final bill differ. Review the work. If you are not satisfied that all of the work was necessary, discuss it. If you are satisfied in this regard, however, don't pull out your wallet just yet. You have one more issue to raise before you pay. "I understand that the work was needed, but what bothers me is the difference between the estimate and the bill. I need to work with people who can give me accurate estimates of cost. I don't want to be put in this position again." At the very least, use this incident as an opportunity to put your mechanic on notice regarding estimates. If he is really interested in your continued patronage, he may even be willing to negotiate the present bill.

When a repair is unsatisfactory or soon fails, resist the temptation to respond angrily. Attack the problem, not the person. Proceed on the assumption that the mechanic wants to do the job correctly, that he wants you to be happy with his work. Don't tell him that he screwed up or did a bad job. Instead, simply report the problem in detail, confirm your understanding that he will fix it promptly, and agree on a delivery time.

Again, most mechanics are professionals who want you as a satisfied client. But there are some—probably more than a few—who will deny that a problem exists even when you confront them with it. I once brought a car in for work, only to discover, when I picked it up, that the steering wheel was now upside down! I pointed this out to the mechanic, who told me something about the worm gear and that the wheel would "adjust itself" in the course of driving.

What do you do in a case like this?

Don't argue. Listen patiently to what he has to say, then tell him that you are not satisfied. Of *course* the steering wheel will not "adjust itself." But don't dispute that. Instead, take the matter up from where his line of reasoning has dropped it: "I don't want to wait for the wheel to adjust itself. I brought the car in with the wheel right side up, and that is the way I want to leave with it. I certainly can't sign off on the repair as is. Please go ahead and adjust the steering wheel now."

Unless you are very knowledgeable about cars, even a poor mechanic knows more than you about how they work. Don't argue about opinions, assessments, or procedures. Instead, state what you are and are not satisfied with. Concentrate on performance as you experience it.

If you fail to resolve your repair problems, resist the impulse either to give up or to vent your anger in idle threats. Tell the mechanic, simply and directly, that you are dissatisfied with the repair work. If the repair shop is part of a dealership, make a point of obtaining from the mechanic the name and telephone number of the individual with whom you can lodge a complaint. If the shop is independent, tell the mechanic that he has left you no choice other than notifying the Better Business Bureau or the appropriate community consumer affairs department.

Words to Use

adequate	judgment
advice	malfunction
agree	necessary
agreement	opinion
careful	optional
cost	performance
deadline	priority
decide	promise
desirable	repair
determine	satisfaction
diagnosis	satisfactory
estimate	satisfied
expedite	schedule
extra	service
failure	time
faulty	unhappy
inadequate	value
inconvenient	worth
judge	

Phrases to Use

accurate estimate	important that it be ready on time
agree on this delivery time	to my satisfaction
assign priority	What is your plan?
call me before you do the work	What is your recommendation?
expedite the work	What would you do?
how much	you promised
how much more	

Words to Avoid

cheated	irresponsible
incompetent	wrong

Phrases to Avoid

doesn't matter
do whatever you have to
I'll sue
it's in your hands
*leave it entirely in your
    hands*
leave it to you
money is no object

poorly done
ripped off
whatever it costs
whenever it's ready
whenever you can
you and I both know
your fault

Your Script

1.

I want a full tune-up, oil change, and lube job. I haven't been having any problems with the car, but do let me know if you see anything. Of course, you'll call me before you do any repair work. When will the car be ready? . . . I'll check in with you about 2 p.m.

A straightforward explanation of what you want and what you expect will help prevent problems later.

2.

The car has been idling rough and often stalls shortly after I start it in the morning, especially if the weather is damp. I want to get it running smoothly and reliably. Of course, you should call me before you actually begin repair work. If I don't hear from you by early afternoon, I'll check in to discuss what needs to be done.

Underscore the necessity of calling you before work is done.

3.

You: *You promised the car by 3 o'clock. I was counting on that. I definitely need the car for this evening. When should I pick it up?*

Mechanic: *I suppose about six.*

You: *That's a lot later than three, and I don't know that I can cut my schedule so close. I've got to use the car to make a call this evening. What can you do to expedite things?*

Promised is a strong word. Use it. Explain the nature of the inconvenience that missing the deadline has caused you. Negotiate for a new deadline.

4.

You: *As I told you over the phone, the car still stalls quite often.*

Mechanic: *That should improve with time. It needs to work itself out.*

You: *Unfortunately, I don't have the time to wait. I need the car to perform well and dependably now. That's why I brought it to you. I'm not satisfied with its performance. I'm not satisfied with the repair work.*

Don't let the mechanic deny your complaint, but don't engage in fruitless technical arguments. Confine your complaint to your dissatisfaction with the automobile's performance. There can be no arguing about that. You are either satisfied or not.

Responses to Anticipate

There's nothing more I can do about it.
Reply with:

☑ *You mean that the car cannot be repaired? Or that you can't repair it? Should I take it elsewhere?*

We've just been so swamped here I couldn't get your car done on time.
Reply with:

☑ *I understand that you've got a lot of cars to take care of. I also have a business to run, and I was counting on picking up my car when you had promised. What can you do to make up for lost time?*

I know I quoted you $450, but, when I started to work, I found a lot more wrong.
Reply with:

☑ *I appreciate that, but the fact is that we had agreed that you would call me before proceeding with repairs that exceeded the estimate. I was not planning to spend this kind of money at this time. I need to work with people who can help me control costs. I can't just trust to luck. I'm not sure I would have okayed all of this work. Let's review the bill.*

The Bill Collector

It happens—and has happened—to most of us at one time or another. We forget to pay a bill. We put off paying a bill. Or we can't pay a bill. The phone rings, and it's "Mr. Smith" or "Mrs. Green" from Master-Card, or Visa, or the local hardware store.

"I'm calling about the outstanding balance due on your account. When do you intend to pay that?"

"Your account shows an unpaid balance of $645.78. We need to get payment on that right away."

"Are you aware of the outstanding balance you have with us? We need to clear that out. When can we expect your check?"

Usually, the call is coolly professional. (There are strict laws nowadays concerning harassment.) Your response to it, however, is usually anything but cool. Depending on your financial condition, your overwhelming impulse is to promise immediate payment. You stammer, hem, haw, then blurt out something like "I'm putting the check into the mail right now." Well, this is actually fine, if you've got the money, and if you are sure that the call was not made in error—that you actually do owe the money.

Generally it is best to fight the shamefaced impulse to make instant amends by promising to run to the mailbox. If finances are, indeed, a problem, the better strategy is to make no promise that will either strap you or that you cannot keep. Instead, buy time. Tell the caller that you are aware of the problem, that you need to review your immediate financial situation, and that you will call back at a specified time. Agree on the time, hang up, then calculate just what you can pay and when. Make sure you return the call as promised.

There is, of course, an even better strategy than this. There is no getting around the fact that difficulty paying bills is a galling problem. Don't compound it by giving your creditors the impression that you are ignoring them, evading them, or generally "blowing them off." When you become aware of an impending problem—when you are going to be late paying a bill, or if you are unable to pay a bill—bite the bullet and make a call. Inform the creditor of your problem, explain it, and propose an alternative payment plan. Negotiate with your creditor before she calls *you*.

Whether you make the call or respond to one, however, be aware that speaking from a painful sense of guilt or shame, promising payments you cannot make or that will simply cause you to default on someone else, solves nothing. Collection callers work on the principle that the squeaky wheel gets the grease. Trouble is, the grease is usually in short supply. The bill collector does not know what your financial circumstances are, and she does not care. Her job is to get you to pay the particular account for which she is responsible. Most bill collectors are authorized and willing to negotiate alternate payment terms with you. Creditors know from bitter experience that delinquent accounts regularly turn into wholly "non-productive" accounts. Unless huge amounts of money are involved, legal action is impractical. The best alternative is to negotiate. Some payment, after all, is better than none.

Owing money makes you feel pretty powerless, and as we have repeatedly noted, it is when you feel weakest that your voice is at its most feeble. It is far easier to speak up from a position of power.

Where can you find that position in this case? Your leverage is in the very fact that you are willing to negotiate with a creditor. You can look at the situation in two ways: You owe, and you cannot pay; or, the creditor wants something you have and is willing to negotiate with you for it. The first point of view makes you weak; the second allows you a measure of strength. The choice is obvious. Therefore, don't throw away your power of negotiation by making careless promises. Talk to your creditor and work out a plan that you have every expectation of living up to.

Focus the conversation *briefly* and in general terms on the reasons for your delinquency. "I've had unexpected medical expenses." "I was out of work." "I've just started a new job." "I've had financial reverses." Then turn to what you propose to pay. My advice is to view this as a genuine negotiation; that is, begin with the lowest numbers and easiest terms you think you can get away with. Work up from there, if necessary, but do not let yourself be talked into making an agreement that you cannot abide by. Two important points need to be added. While you should not act from a sense of embarrassment—caving in with lavish apologies and unreasonable promises—neither should you go to the other extreme of responding arrogantly: "You want your money? Well, why don't you just do something about it?" When you owe, groveling is not called for, but a tone of businesslike courtesy is. Do not communicate shame or embarrassment, but do communicate your desire to settle the account as expeditiously as your circumstances permit.

Words to Use

accommodate	*expeditious*
alternatives	*feasible*
apologize	*grateful*
appreciate	*inconvenience*
cashflow	*manageable*
cooperate	*overlooked*
difficulty	*pay*
efficient	*plan*
emergency	*problem*

reasonable
resolve
schedule
send
settle
sorry

temporary
together
understanding
unreasonable
work
workable

Phrases to Use

*experiencing cash flow
    problems*
explore some alternatives
formulate a payment plan
get this settled quickly
make us both happy
reach an agreement
reach a workable solution
*resolve this as quickly as
    possible*

soon be resolved
suggest some alternatives
temporary problem
unanticipated expenses
unanticipated reserves
unexpected expenses
unexpected losses
work together

Words to Avoid

can't
fault
immediately
no

sue
tough
won't
wrong

Phrases to Avoid

do something about it
I cannot pay
I forgot
I have no money
I'm broke
I'm very, very sorry
I never got a bill
it's in the mail

it's not my fault
it won't happen again
right away
sue me
victim of circumstance
you're out of luck
*you've come to the wrong
    person*

Your Script

1.

My name is Mary Smith, and my account number is 123-456-789. I'm calling to advise you that I'm going to be late with this month's payment. I had some unexpected emergency expenses. It's a temporary problem, and I will be able to send the payment by the twenty-fifth. I would greatly appreciate it if you could accommodate me.

Despite a natural tendency to avoid one's creditors, by far the best strategy is to keep lines of communication open and to speak to your creditors in advance of a late or missed payment. Don't beg, don't grovel. Make a polite business proposition. Most creditors are willing to accommodate you.

2.

My name is Mary Smith, and my account number is 123-456-789. I am experiencing cash flow problems that are going to make it difficult or impossible for me to pay my bill in full. I'd like to discuss some alternatives with you.

Again, communicate before the account becomes delinquent. Take the initiative. Most creditors are willing to negotiate.

3.

Collector: *Your account is sixty days overdue. When can we expect a payment?*

You: *Yes, I realize that it is overdue. I am experiencing some financial problems. Let me review my situation and call you back tomorrow morning at this time. I'll be able to give you a firm date then.*

If possible, secure time to formulate a realistic payment plan.

4.

Collector: *I'm calling about your overdue account. We need payment on it now.*

You: *I've had some financial difficulties. Please let me review my current situation and call you back at this time tomorrow morning. I'll have a suggestion for an alternative payment schedule.*

Collector: *My supervisor won't let me do that. I need a response from you now.*

You: *I agree that the money is due you, and I would like to arrive at a workable plan to get the account settled as quickly as possible. I cannot do that responsibly on the spur of the moment, however. Please be assured that I will call you. If you are having a problem with your supervisor, why don't you let me speak to him or her?*

Don't let the assertion of "company policy" or other problems deter you. Be cooperative and explain why you need time.

5.

Collector: *When you purchased the Acme Rug Beater you made a promise to pay. You are not living up to that promise, and we will have to file a bad credit report and send our lawyers after you if you don't pay immediately.*

You: *I am eager to settle this account. I have, however, suffered some financial reverses and am experiencing a temporary cash flow problem. Before you take any further action, please let me review my financial situation and call you back with a plan.*

Meet anger and bullying with calm and assurance.

6.

My name is Mary Smith, and my account number is 123-456-789. We spoke yesterday about my account. I've looked at my finances, and I've come up with an alternative repayment schedule I know I can manage. Here is what I suggest . . .

Be sure to make the call that you promised to make.

Responses to Anticipate

A thing like this can really damage your credit rating.
Reply with:

☑ *I am very aware of that—which is why I would appreciate your willingness to work out an alternative payment schedule.*

It's admirable that you want to make some payment, but what you suggest is just not enough. We can't accept your proposal.
Reply with:

☑ *Unfortunately, it's what I can afford at present. Can you suggest an alternative? I do want to settle this account, but I don't want to make empty promises.*

We'll have to call in our lawyers.
Reply with:

☑ *I understand your concern about my account. I was hoping that my suggested alternative schedule would make legal action unnecessary. What is your objection to my plan?*

The Car Salesperson

Is there anyone more maligned than the automobile salesperson? Most of us enjoy buying a new car—or a good used car—but dread doing battle with the salesperson. We expect to be pressured, fast talked, and even deceived, and we go into the transaction keyed up with either anxiety or an inordinate thirst for blood. Whether we feel threatened or aggressive, these hostile feelings are not generally conducive to speaking up in a way that will secure you the best car at the best price.

Make no mistake, I am not advising you to let your guard down when you go in to purchase a car. This is a high-stakes game, and while most sales people are honest and thoroughly professional, they all work on a commission based on the actual sales price. Worse, a sizable minority of auto sales personnel are more or less deficient in scruples. But the object is not to outsmart the salesperson. Rather, the object of negotiating for an automobile is to *buy the car you want at the best price you can get*. Focus on the car, not on the personality of the individual from whom you are buying it.

Speaking up in this case, then, involves preparation. Research the available cars in your price range—the various consumer-oriented automobile magazines and such publications as *Consumer Reports* are good places to start—and decide, before you enter the showroom, what you want and approximately how much you are willing to pay. The more you know, the better off you are. In this case, effective communication depends on preparation. The publishers of the popular consumer-related magazines also produce good booklength guides to buying automobiles. Arming yourself with hard knowledge gleaned from such sources will make it far easier to focus on the real object of your quest—the car—rather than on the salesperson. The more you know about the car, the less you need to rely on your ability to assess the honesty and integrity of the stranger with whom you have to deal.

Buying a car is similar to making that fancy consumer electronics purchase—only it is even more intense. Cars appeal simultaneously to childlike fantasies and to an adult sense of self-indulgence. People really do fall in love with cars. The smells of the new vehicles, the bright lights of the showroom—these are seductive indeed, and your impulse is to buy and buy now.

If you want to communicate effectively, fight the impulse. Purchasing an automobile is no time for an exercise in impulse buying. Make your initial visits to *several* showrooms with a determination *not* to buy. Talk to the salespeople and get their names and numbers. Scope out the best deals. Then, only after you have gathered your data, return to the dealership. Use the best price you were quoted as a starting point for an even better price. And if you have a car to trade, do not even bring up that subject until *after* you have been quoted a satisfactory price. Hold it in reserve.

Now comes the hard part. If you and the salesperson are far apart, use your most powerful nonverbal weapon: your feet. Walk away from the deal. Unless the price gap is very wide, chances are that the salesperson will follow you. If he or she does not, and you don't find a better deal elsewhere, call back—on the telephone, not in person. Ask for the salesperson you had spoken to earlier: "This is Sarah Williams. We spoke about that Saab 9000. Have you given any further thought to price? I'd offered $22,500 and you were at $27,000." See what happens.

It can be difficult to keep your head when purchasing a car. Prepare yourself by researching the appropriate automobiles, and focus on the car rather than the salesperson. The salesperson has emotional power over you; he has something you want. But *you* have it within your power to help that salesperson make a living. All he offers is a car. You offer sustenance. There's no contest.

Words to Use

alternatives	discuss
ballpark	lowest
best	negotiate
careful	options
comparison	select
deal	value

Phrases to Use

Do you want to sell the car?	quite a bit more than I want to spend
How firm is that price?	
I have been looking	real price
I'm listening	sticker price
not an adequate value	tell me what you can offer
not good enough	Where can we go from here?

Words to Avoid

absolute	immediately
excited	now
fair	terrific
good	wonderful
great	

Phrases to Avoid

can't wait	trade-in allowance
right away	What will you take in trade?
the *price*	

Your Script

1.

I have been looking at midsize sedans under $25,000 and thought I'd give the Taurus a closer look. I'm interested in safety, fuel economy, and styling—pretty much in that order. What can you tell me about the car?

Use the salesperson. Come in having done your homework, but do let her speak, let her sell. Make it clear that you are in the process of evaluating a purchase ("I have been looking").

2.

Salesperson: *I cannot give it to you for less than $24,500. To be perfectly frank, the margin's just not there.*

You: *Okay. We're $3,000 apart. I'm willing to split the difference.*

Negotiate—not in terms of personality, but strictly in terms of numbers, extras, and value.

3.

Salesperson: *No can do. I really am giving you my best price.*

You: *I appreciate that. Why don't you give me your card, and if I don't do better elsewhere, I'll probably be calling on you again.*

When she won't budge, it's time for you to get moving. Leave—but in a friendly, unhurried way. This is no time for dramatics. You want to convince the salesperson that you are literally walking away from the deal—at least for now.

Responses to Anticipate

You're making it tough on me.

Reply with:

☑ *I don't want to make it tough on anybody. I just want to spend as little on this car as possible.*

I wish we could do business—but if you haven't got the money, you haven't got the money.

Reply with:

☑ *Well, I have your card. I'm going to look around some more.*

You're not going to get a better deal than this.

Reply with:

☑ *There's only one way for me to find out, I guess. I've got your card. If you turn out to be right, I'll give you a call.*

The Coworker

Office politics are complex and varied, subject to the number of persons involved, questions of seniority, the relative prosperity of the business, the role of management, and the nature of the business, among many other factors. Despite this variety, there are universal principles for establishing effective communication between you and your colleagues.

The first principle is so obvious that it bears careful examination and exploration: *Respect your coworker.* In general terms, this means that you should follow the biblical injunction to do unto others as you would have others do unto you. In more specific terms, it means you should listen to your coworkers, hear what they say, and demonstrate that you have heard them and that you value their words. Punctuate conversations with such phrases as, "That's interesting," "It's worth thinking about," "I like that," and so on. You can establish a climate of respect through language like this.

The second principle: *Establish ground rules and discuss and refine them as often as necessary.* It is surprising how many companies squander—and annoy—their work-force assets by apportioning responsibilities poorly. Make sure that you and your coworkers understand your jobs. If management defines them poorly, take over. Discuss and define your responsibilities—and don't be afraid to redefine them in accordance with the changing demands of your business.

The third principle: *When necessary, sound your horn.* I drove a car in London once. I thought that the most difficult thing would be remembering to drive on the left side of the road. Actually, the biggest problem turned out to be the fact that people over there rarely sound their horns. They're just too polite. In fact, they're so polite, they would sooner ram into you than give you a warning beep. Learn how to avoid an unpleasant—or even disastrous—encounter with your coworkers by sounding your horn as necessary. If something bothers you, let it be known calmly but firmly. If a coworker treads on your turf, let her know: "Susan, just a minute. That's my responsibility, and I'll take care of it."

The fourth principle: *Use small talk in a big way.* Coffee-break and lunchtime conversation is valuable. Use it for the informal discussion of ideas, or use it to demonstrate your interest in your coworkers—their families, their hobbies, their activities outside of work. The more you know about a person, the more rounded your image of his character, the easier it is to respect him and to elicit his respect for you. Small talk builds relationships, morale, and company personality—the sense that you are all in business together to achieve common goals and obtain mutual benefits.

Most situations in which you are intimidated by a coworker—situations in which you cannot speak up—can be traced to a failure of at least two of these principles. To be sure, adhering to them provides no guarantee of a conflict-free and productive working atmosphere. But failure to adhere to them does virtually guarantee a corporate climate that ranges from unpleasant to catastrophic.

Words to Use

advice	*facilitate*
advise	*fascinated*
aid	*great*
apologize	*harmful*
appropriate	*hear*
assignment	*help*
assist	*helpful*
concerned	*impede*
conclude	*inappropriate*
consider	*interested*
cooperate	*participate*
counsel	*plan*
damaging	*respect*
discuss	*responsibility*
enjoy	*responsive*
enthusiastic	*review*
evaluate	*share*
examine	*sorry*
excellence	*unintentional*
excellent	*value*
expedite	*weigh*

Phrases to Use

don't find this helpful	*I'll attend to it*
find this helpful	*let me know what I can do*

*let me hear what you have
    to say*
let me think about that
let's reconsider
let's weigh the options
listen to you
not your responsibility
seek your advice

seek your counsel
share your ideas with us
that's a good idea
this is not very helpful
this makes it more difficult
value your opinion
want to hear

Words to Avoid

can't
demand
fail
insist

must
no
won't

Phrases to Avoid

bad idea
*I don't want to listen to any
    other ideas*
*I think we've had enough
    discussion*
I've heard enough
mind your own business
this is not the way to do it

this won't work
*those kinds of things never
    work*
What's wrong with you?
you can't
you'd better not
you have it all wrong
you must do

Your Script

1.

I'm very interested in hearing your ideas on how we should go about preparing the year-end report. There's certainly need for improvement, and I think we need to look as good as we possibly can.

Express openness and a sense of teamwork and common cause.

2.

Your idea is interesting, but I'm not sure it will work. We tried something very similar two years ago, and nobody was very happy about it. I hope you can give it some further thought, because I need all the help I can get.

Reject a bad idea without rejecting the person who has offered it.

3.

I have to tell you, George, that I was upset to hear that you revised my sales report without consulting me. I've looked at the report and I agree with the revisions, but it was not appropriate to make the changes without some discussion. I appreciate your advice and your input, but, in the future, let's sit down and discuss any revisions you might think necessary.

The word *inappropriate* is very useful to defuse competitive, potentially destructive situations. Build your complaint around similar words that address the issue rather than the personalities involved. Also note the stress here on the "future." Rather than say something provocative like "Don't let it happen again," point out in a positive way that you will continue to work together.

Responses to Anticipate

Just because something didn't work last year doesn't mean it won't work now.

Reply with:

☑ *You're right. We should discuss all the possibilities and consider what may be different now. But, frankly, I don't think that what you are suggesting is the answer.*

I'm sorry if I stepped out of line, but there just wasn't time to discuss the matter.

Reply with:

☑ *I think this kind of thing is important enough to make time for.*

The Contractor

Any number of books and videos on home maintenance and home remodeling will give you the same very good piece of advice: When you work with a contractor, begin by putting everything in writing. As Yogi Berra once said, a verbal contract ain't worth the paper it's written on.

It's true, the contract is important legal protection, and it gives you something to refer to if the contractor fails to perform as promised. ("The contract specifies that molding and trim are included.") I would not employ a contractor who balked at putting the job's specs in writing. When a father-and-son team once objected to my request for a contract by telling me that the family had worked sixty years in my town and had an untarnished reputation, I replied, "I'm sure that's true. But *I've* known you only about fifteen minutes." And I took the job elsewhere.

Necessary though it is, a good, clear contract does not make effective, ongoing verbal communication superfluous. The object is to keep the job going smoothly and catch any potential glitches before they become major problems. Once you have established your contract, underscore verbally that your first concerns are quality and adhering to the specified schedule. Invite the contractor to speak to you as often as necessary in the course of the job, and let him know that you intend to speak to him as needed: "I'm a strong believer in communication. I have no intention of telling you how to do your job. I know you're going to do a great job. But I want a terrific result at the end of all this, so I will be asking you questions and seeking your advice pretty frequently."

As you monitor the work, express your satisfaction as the job warrants. If something doesn't look right, don't immediately accuse or criticize, but ask questions: "How does this gap get filled in? What will it look like?" "How are we doing on the schedule?" Always focus your questions and remarks on the job, not on the contractor personally. While you may often feel that your relationship with the contractor is adversarial, it is imperative to communicate to him a feeling that you are, indeed, on the same team. You both want a good result, a job well done. When things are not going as you would like them to, stress teamwork rather than vent your frustration in accusations and threats.

Words to Use

agreement	question
ask	reasons
complaints	redo
cooperate	review
correct	revise
discuss	satisfaction
happy	satisfactory
improve	satisfied
job	schedule
plan	together
priority	unhappy
problems	unsatisfactory
quality	

Phrases to Use

behind schedule	redo as specified in the contract
How will you . . .?	
next step	review the contract

review the schedule
schedule slipping
set priorities for the rest of
    the job
suspending payment

this is unsatisfactory
    because
very pleased with this
What will you . . .?
When will you . . .?

Words to Avoid

alarmed
bad
disappointed
disaster
hopeless

incompetent
miserable
slow
sue

Phrases to Avoid

all bets are off
bad job
don't bother me
don't come to me with
    questions
I can't believe how bad this
    is

I leave it entirely to you
I trust you
that's why I hired you
use your own judgment
won't get a cent
won't pay
you're the expert

Your Script

1.

So, now that we've got everything written down, I just want to underscore three points: I'm interested in getting the very highest quality you can give me, and I expect the work to be completed within the time frame we have agreed on. Also, I'm a great believer in communication. If you have any questions or you want me to take a look at anything, please don't hesitate to ask. In turn, I'll probably have a good many questions for you as the project moves on. I know you'll give me a great job.

Set up an open relationship from the start. Let the contractor know that you are deeply interested in the work.

2.

You: *The gap between the trim and this wall is awfully wide. What's the plan for closing this up?*

Contractor: *We'll take care of it.*

You: *How do you do that? I'm concerned.*

Contractor: *Leave it to us.*

You: *I intend to. But it's not something I expected, and I'd like to know how you intend to cope with it.*

When something looks wrong, questions are better than accusations, which soon result in fruitless argument. Persist until your questions are answered.

3.

You: *The contract calls for primer-sealer on all raw wood surfaces. I see you're about to start right in with the paint.*

Contractor: *Well, primer-sealer really isn't necessary. It will go faster if we just start painting.*

You: *You and I both want the best job possible. That's why we agreed to use primer-sealer. I want to stick to the specs we agreed on.*

Use the contract not as a cudgel but as an index to evaluate performance. Keep the contractor on your team through liberal use of the pronoun *we*.

Responses to Anticipate

I'm the expert. That's why you hired me. Leave it to me.
Reply with:

☑ *You are the expert, but I have to live here, and I really want to be happy with this job. I know I'll be happy with the job if I am satisfied that we didn't misunderstand each other at any point.*

I know I'm running late. There isn't much I can do about it.
Reply with:

☑ *This is not what we had hoped for. What's your best estimate on finishing up?*

I did the best I could. It can't be done better.
Reply with:

☑ *Let me review the project and make note of what I need to be done—or redone—before I release the balance of the money due.*

The Customer Complaint Clerk

This is a book about communicating—using language to achieve certain goals that often prove elusive because we fail to speak up. When you return a defective or unwanted item for a refund or exchange, however, it is usually best to begin by saying as little as possible. Most of us go to the return counter at least vaguely expecting an argument, but the fact is that the majority of customer complaint clerks are trained *not* to dispute customer claims, but simply to process the return, refund, repair, or exchange. Approach the clerk with this assumption.

> *"I am returning this for a refund."*
>
> *"This is defective. I want to exchange it."*

At most, you may be asked what the problem is. If so, state it as simply as you can. "The glass is cracked." "It won't work in reverse." "The switch sticks." This is usually enough.

What do you do on those relatively rare occasions when you do get an argument?

You persevere calmly. You do not attack the clerk, but concentrate instead on the item you wish to return or replace, always emphasizing your dissatisfaction with it. If necessary, you speak to the manager. In any case, you do not yield the floor—or your place at the head of the line—until you get satisfaction.

Words to Use

customer	*problem*
defective	*reputation*
dissatisfied	*resolve*
faulty	*satisfaction*
guarantee	*service*
inoperative	*unhappy*
malfunction	

Phrases to Use

cannot accept	*not satisfied with*
defective item	*nothing less*
defective merchandise	*poorly made*
merchant's reputation	*resolve the problem*
not happy with	*return for a full refund*

Words to Avoid

cheated	*lawyer*
demand	*sue*
junk	

Phrases to Avoid

gyp joint	*you don't know who you're dealing with*
hear from my attorney	
I'll have your job	*you're in big trouble*

Your Script

1.

I'm returning this defective coffee maker. Please exchange it for one that works.

Nine times out of ten—or even better—this is all it takes. Offer no more explanation than you have to.

2.

You: *The air conditioner makes a great deal of noise and does not cool adequately.*

Clerk (after testing): *I don't find anything wrong with it.*

You: *I am not satisfied with the unit. It's louder than any air conditioner I've ever had, and it performs poorly.*

Clerk: *I can't take it back unless there's something wrong with it.*

You: *It is defective, and I cannot accept it. Please call the manager here.*

Clerk: *It's not something I want to bother him with. There really is nothing wrong with the air conditioner.*

You: *I notice that you have a good many people in line here. I'm sure they are getting tired of my complaining about the defective product you don't want to take responsibility for. Please ask the manager to come here so that we can resolve this.*

Manager: *My clerk says that he tested the air conditioner and found nothing wrong.*

You: *Can you guarantee that the test is absolutely accurate?*

Manager: *It's always been.*

You: *In this case, it has failed. I would not trudge back here with this unit if it was working. I am inclined to buy a different unit here—if you'll take this back and give me a credit slip without further delay.*

Calm persistence is called for. If you can offer the clerk or manager some incentive—such as your continued patronage—do so.

Responses to Anticipate

It's against company policy to make a cash refund. We will give you credit.

Reply with:

☑ *That's not acceptable. You make no such statement on the bill of sale. Please get the manager, so that I can take up the matter with him or her.*

You'll have to wait three to four weeks for the refund to go through.
Reply with:

☑ *Considering the amount of inconvenience I've already suffered, I'm not in the mood to wait. Please get your manager over here to explain the reason for the delay to me.*

The Doctor or Dentist

Too often we take ourselves to our doctor or dentist the way we take a sputtering automobile to a garage or a malfunctioning appliance to the shop. We present ourselves for repair. We tell the doctor or dentist what hurts, and then, responding more to the trappings of the profession—white coat, diplomas, and stainless steel—than to the woman or man we have called on, we are silent.

Take over, doc. I'm all yours.

The truth is that few medical and dental professionals today encourage this kind of unquestioning reliance on their powers. Most welcome more communication with their patients, though three things continue to interfere with this. First, many practitioners either cannot or do not make sufficient time for unhurried conversation with their patients. Second, many practitioners lack the skills that foster full communication with their patients. Third, many (probably most) patients have yet to catch up with the trend that encourages two-way communication with the health-care professional. As many continue to see it, the woman or man in a white coat does not merely occupy a pedestal; he or she exists on an entirely different plane from mere mortals. Paradoxically, for many of us, it is hardest to communicate with the person who holds our life and health in her hands. This, of course, is the person with whom we should communicate most freely and effectively.

There are a number of very fine popular books on what to ask your doctor. Perusing one or more of these—see, for example, Justus J. Schifferes's *Family Medical Encyclopedia* (Pocket Books, 1977) or Dr. Stuart M. Berger's *What Your Doctor Didn't Learn in Medical School* (Avon Books, 1988)—is good preparation for effective communication with your doctor *or* your dentist. You may then want to jot down any issues you wish to raise during your visit. It also helps to prepare your frame of mind. Remember, your health-care professional wants to help you, wants you to be healthy, to find relief, to be satisfied. To be sure, doctors and dentists are usually well paid and are as interested in making money as anyone else. However, the cynical view that money is their exclusive focus is rarely valid. Most health-care professionals are primarily motivated by a desire to heal. Nowadays, most are also trained to believe that what the patient tells them is as valuable to diagnosis as any high-tech test. They also learn that effective communication shapes a patient's attitude, and attitude, of course, profoundly affects the process of healing or failing to heal.

There is no guarantee that your practitioner is motivated in this way or that he has taken all he has learned to heart; however, the chances are that your health-care professional is far more ready to hear you than you may realize. Begin with this assumption: Effective communication is an important part of diagnosis and treatment. Moreover, your doctor or dentist is well aware of this.

But what happens when you feel that communication is breaking down?

In this case you have a golden opportunity to educate your practitioner. Tell her what makes you uncomfortable. "Doctor, I have every confidence in you, but I don't feel as if we're communicating effectively. I don't get the sense that you hear what I'm saying." If possible, be even more specific: "You haven't answered my last question." Doctors and dentists sometimes seem to filter out questions they consider either irrelevant or for which they simply have no ready answer. Don't hesitate to point out any question that remains unaddressed. However, be prepared for the possibility that your practitioner has no answer, and if she does tell you that she cannot answer the question, don't be deterred from exploring it further: "Why can't you answer it?"

A call on your doctor is no time for passivity, but neither is it an occasion for combativeness. Instead, make the visit interactive—a learning experience for you as well as your practitioner.

Words to Use

appreciate	*happy*
communicate	*hear*
concerned	*impression*
depressed	*listen*
discomfort	*nervous*
explain	*obscure*
feel	*pain*
frightened	*repeat*
fully	*sense*

talk
unclear
understand

unhappy
upset
worried

Phrases to Use

How should we proceed?
I am concerned about
I don't feel
I feel
I get the impression
it seems to me
I want you to hear
let me tell you
please address

please answer
please consider
what bothers me is
What about?
What do you recommend?
What do you suggest?
What should we do?
What's the next step?
you don't seem

Words to Avoid

incompetent

irresponsible

Phrases to Avoid

do what you want
if that's what you think
if you say it's not important,
    it's not important
I'm all yours
it's okay with me

it's up to you
tell me what to do
whatever you think best
What should I do?
You have to tell me.
you're the doctor

Your Script

Something is bothering me, which I've been meaning to talk to you about. I occasionally get the impression that you don't always hear what I'm saying to you. For example, when I mentioned that the medication you prescribed does alleviate the pain, but I sometimes feel sort of light-headed and disoriented, you just said that you were glad the medication was effective. I like the medication, and I can live with the side effects—if they aren't going to get worse. It's something I'd like us to talk about.

Be as clear about your feelings concerning the state of communication between you and your practitioner as you are about the symptoms that brought you to her in the first place. Address these issues as soon as possible. When you can, introduce the plural pronoun (*we, us, our*) in order to keep the relationship interactive even at the most basic linguistic level.

Response to Anticipate

Those symptoms are irrelevant to the main problem.
Reply with:

☑ *I understand that they may be irrelevant to you, but they are very relevant to me. What can we do about them?*

Let me take care of it.
Reply with:

☑ *I have great confidence in you, but it will make me feel much better if I have a full sense of acting from a basis of complete information. So, please, let's discuss it.*

I wish I had enough time to talk at greater length.
Reply with:

☑ *Doctor, I appreciate that you are very busy. That's why I am particularly grateful for your taking a few extra moments to explain this to me again.*

You have to trust me.
Reply with:

☑ *I do trust you. If I didn't, I wouldn't be here. But my trusting you does not depend on my remaining ignorant of all the options available to me.*

Your Child's Doctor or Dentist

Speaking up to your child's doctor or dentist is, if anything, more difficult than communicating effectively with your own practitioner. When you visit the doctor for yourself, at most you are faced with having to overcome your own aversion to challenging your physician and possibly addressing his deficiencies in the area of communication. But when you take your child to a doctor or dentist, you are pulled by several emotional demands. You have to be a responsible parent and "do what's best for" your child. But who is to decide that? You? The doctor? You also have to be a *responsive* parent, sensitive to your child's needs and fears. You have to be the child's interpreter and advocate, an intermediary between him and the practitioner. And you have to be aware of a natural (and healthy) tendency to resist the efforts of another adult authority figure to take charge of your child's welfare. It is difficult to "relinquish"—in any degree—your child to the care of even a very trusted health-care professional.

In fact, there is nothing you can do to overcome these conflicting feelings. I don't think taking a child to a doctor or dentist—even for "just a check-up"—can ever be a comfortable experience for a parent. But, as we have learned elsewhere in this book, you can communicate effectively in spite of strong feelings.

As when you prepare to visit your own doctor, arm yourself with as much information as you can. Such books as *Dr. Spock's Baby and Child Care* (Dutton, 1985) and The Boston Children's Hospital's *The New Child Health Encyclopedia* (Delta, 1987) are good popular sources that will give you a leg up on communicating efficiently with your child's doctor. In addition, a number of children's books are available to prepare your child for the visit. These may make things easier for both of you.

The enlightened practitioner makes every effort to listen to your child, but he realizes that you are his primary source of information. If any relationship calls for a spirit of cooperation and teamwork, this is it. Don't "bring" your child to the doctor. Don't "deliver" her into the hands of a dentist. Visit the practitioner with your child, and work with the practitioner to do what you both agree is best for the child. Shape your communication to reflect and reinforce the sense of cooperative, collaborative effort. "What is our next step?" "What do you suggest we do?" "What are our options?" "We want to do what's best. How do you think we should proceed?"

Teamwork precludes passivity, but it also rules out provocative challenge. This includes such exclamations as, "I want the best for my child." "You give him the best treatment you can." Of course, your practitioner assumes *you* want the best. But such statements are not superfluous; they are downright harmful. Use *I* and *you* very sparingly in situations where *we* and *us* are called for: "Of course, we both want to do what's best for Bill." This is not a challenge, tinged with an edge of aggression and doubt, but a statement of solidarity—something you can both agree on.

Words to Use

advice	*opinion*
advise	*options*
alternatives	*our*
best	*plan*
choice	*procedure*
consultation	*we*

Phrases to Use

Any suggestions?	*What do you suggest?*
our alternatives	*what our options are*
we want to do what's best	*what we should do*
what course we could take	*Where do we go from here?*
What do you advise?	

Words to Avoid

must   *orders*

Phrases to Avoid

I want what's best   *you better do a good job*
this is how I want it done

Your Script

1.

You: *Do you want to tell the doctor what's wrong?*
Child: *No.*

You: *Well, let me know if I've got this right. Doctor, he's been complaining about an earache in his right ear, and he has been very irritable. He has been running a slight fever—just shy of 100. I know that he also wants me to tell you that he doesn't like needles.*

To whatever degree possible, include your child in the discussion with the practitioner. When you speak for him, invite his comments and corrections.

2.

Doctor: *I am going to prescribe antibiotics.*

You: *Is that our only alternative at this point? She does seem to be getting better. I know we don't want this thing to develop into a full-blown infection, but I'm concerned about overmedicating with antibiotics. Is this really our best course?*

Doctor: *I usually like to attack these things before they get worse, but I understand your concern.*

You: *How should we proceed, then?*

Doctor: *I'll write the prescription. Why don't we wait five days before filling it. If you see improvement, let's hold off. If it seems to be getting worse, go ahead and have it filled. But if it's not cleared up in five days, even if it seems a little better, you'd better fill the prescription.*

You: *That seems like a good plan. Then we are agreed.*

Yes, the doctor does know more about medicine than you do. However, you owe it to your child—and to the working team of your child, your practitioner, and yourself—to make your concerns clear. Note the emphasis on *we* throughout, which stresses collaboration and which helps keep the situation from becoming a confrontation or challenge to authority.

Responses to Anticipate

I'm doing the best thing for your child.
Reply with:

☑ *We both want to do what's best. That's why I need to know what our choices are.*

Quite frankly, you should do what I recommend.
Reply with:

☑ *I agree that what you suggest is probably our best course. Naturally, we both want what's best for Jim, so before we proceed, I'd like to secure one more opinion.*

Do you think he understands my explanation?
Reply with:

☑ *He's old enough to be told what's going on. Why don't you explain the situation fully to me again, and I'll see to it that Sam understands us.*

Your Child's Teacher

We hear a great deal these days about how teachers, who perform one of the most important services in an enlightened society, are not only poorly paid but command precious little respect—from students, parents, and others. That may, unfortunately, be true in the abstract, but the situation is less predictable when it's your kid and his teacher. Whenever I talk to my child's teacher I am aware of straddling two extremes, neither of which is productive of good communication. I either feel like a kid myself, finding it difficult to talk to the teacher as an equal, or I feel excessively defensive about my child and verge on saying things like, "He's just too imaginative for conventional educators," or something even more offensive.

The obstacle to effective communication, as usual, is inappropriate focus. Whether your approach is elaborately deferential or aggressively defensive, you are focusing on yourself instead of on your child and how you can collaborate with his teacher to give him the best educational experience possible. The object is not to prove the teacher wrong, nor to "stand up for" your child, but to create a collaborative climate in which everyone involved—you, the teacher, and (especially) your child—will flourish.

Holding this focus is not always easy. If you are called in to a conference to discuss a problem—behavioral or academic—it is difficult *not* to feel attacked. After all, the personality and intellectual abilities of your offspring are being called into question. It's as if *you* are being accused: of inattention, of setting a bad example, of watching too much TV, of not listening to the right kind of music, of having the wrong kinds of books or none at all, or of simply possessing faulty genes. This is one of those unfortunate situations in which you can do very little to change these quite painful feelings. You don't, however, need to act on the basis of them. Instead, force yourself to focus on the educational transaction among teacher, student, and parent. Demonstrate verbally that you are eager to work collaboratively with the teacher in order to address whatever problem she is calling to your attention.

It is a good plan to nurture this spirit of collaboration in a context other than crisis. Don't wait for a problem to occasion a parent-teacher conference, but try to arrange one or two conferences on your own during the school year to discuss your child and collaborative strategies for furthering his education.

All of this is well and good, but what happens when you are absolutely convinced that the teacher is wrong, that your child is being short-changed intellectually or treated unfairly? Doesn't there come a time to stand up and defend your child?

The answer is a qualified "yes." Certainly you must not let your child suffer second-rate education or unfair treatment. But rather than give in to the temptation to approach the teacher as an adversary, try to hang on to the notion of collaboration. In this case, however, you will have to take even more of the initiative by educating the educator. Review the situation with her and freely offer your insights and suggestions—in a spirit of imparting information rather than doing battle.

This can be very difficult. Teachers, after all, are human beings, subject to the same emotions, fits of temper, lapses of judgment, and prejudices as anyone else. Thrust into continual close contact with a group of children day after day, the teacher is, in fact, the focus of more emotional pressure than most of us. She may be wrong, very wrong, about your child. By no means should you let that pass; however, it may help you to adopt a more constructive attitude toward the situation if you appreciate the conditions that contribute to her misjudgment. Your object is not to defeat the teacher but to help your child and his teacher work more effectively together.

Words to Use

assist	*plan*
collaborate	*positive*
communicate	*practice*
contribute	*promote*
discipline	*reinforce*
educate	*strategy*
encourage	*study*
experience	*understanding*
facilitate	

Phrases to Use

collaborate with you	*positive reinforcement*
facilitate your work	*share my insight with you*
formulate a plan	*share my understanding of*
help you	*the problem*
meet with you regularly	*work with you*

Words to Avoid

bored	*punish*
compel	*unimaginative*
force	*unreasonable*
incompetent	*wrong*
intolerant	*wrong-headed*
mistaken	

Phrases to Avoid

do your job	*What's wrong with her?*
I can't handle him myself.	*you do something about it*
I don't have all day for a	*you don't understand*
conference	*you don't understand my*
I give up	*child*
I leave his education to you	*you know better than I do*
my child is too imaginative	*you're going about it wrong*
for this school	*you're the teacher*

Your Script

1.

I appreciate your seeing me. I wanted to meet with you near the be-

ginning of the school year, mainly to let you know that I am available whenever you might want to talk to me. You've got a very difficult job, and I'd like to do whatever I can to make it easier. We both want the best for Alison. Do you have any general recommendations for things I might be able to do at home?

A get-acquainted conversation can do much to establish a climate of collaboration that may avert problems and that will make it easier to deal with any problems that do occur.

2.

Teacher: *I've asked you here because George is habitually misbehaving in class. He tends to lash out at other children and often disrupts the class. I want you to be aware of this, and I wonder if you can shed any light on it.*

You: *I appreciate your calling me in. Perhaps if you can give me some specific examples of George's misbehavior, I'd have a clearer idea of the problem and we could work together to formulate a strategy for improving his behavior.*

Teacher: *It's difficult to pin down any single incident. It's more a case of general disruptiveness.*

You: *He is certainly a demonstrative child. I've been aware of that for a long time. I still don't have a clear notion of what you consider disruptive, though.*

Teacher: *Well, for example, he talks out of turn. He makes jokes at inappropriate times.*

You: *Is there an appropriate time when he might be encouraged to do these things? You seem to be saying that, thus far, a negative approach hasn't been very effective. Perhaps he needs an opportunity to express himself in a way that the classroom routine doesn't allow. Would you like me to explore this with him?*

This conversation will continue. Help the teacher define the problem. He may see it in a new and more constructive light; in any case, you certainly need to understand it as fully as possible. Make an effort to get beyond abstractions—not with the object of compelling the teacher to *prove* his case against your child, but with the goal of exploring the issues more thoroughly together. Rather than challenging the teacher to do something about the problem, ask how you can help.

Responses to Anticipate

I'm not asking you to do my job.
Reply with:

☑ *Believe me, your job is more than I want to handle. I'm just suggesting that we explore ways in which his experience at home can supplement what you do here.*

To be quite frank, he is a very frustrating child.
Reply with:

☑ *Feeling frustrated makes it hard to do the job you've got to do. Have you any suggestions about how I might be able to help? What can I do at home? Can we work to arrive at a plan?*

She's headed for big trouble.
Reply with:

☑ *I don't find it very helpful to be told this. I appreciate that there is a problem. Rather than put it all on her, though, why don't we discuss the nature of the problem and, together, arrive at some strategies for helping her with it?*

The IRS Auditor

There is a little room in the back of the mind of every American taxpayer reserved for Audit Angst. Some time in April, I find myself in a bookstore, furtively thumbing through the indexes of various income-tax guides under the word *audit*. Each year I comfort myself with audit statistics published in these books: relatively few people get audited—maybe 2 to 4 percent, depending on income and the nature of employment.

But what if it does actually happen?

The books I peruse in the bookstore at tax time say things like, "An IRS notice of examination is not a cause for panic." I disagree.

Actually, it's as good a cause for panic as any. The point is that panic will do you no good. If you get a notice of examination, respond to it promptly. If you have a tax preparer, she should accompany you to the audit. If you prepared the return yourself, you should get ready for the audit by reading any of the solid popular income tax guides available, and you should review the return, paying special attention to any specific items called into question; you should gather and photocopy all relevant backup material, including receipts and other proofs of the legitimacy of your deductions; and, finally, you should picture yourself at the interview.

Run through it in your mind. Try to think about and jot down the possible questions. Contemplate answers to them. Imagine the agent as a perfectly ordinary person, a person with a job to do—and nothing more. These days, the IRS is particularly sensitive to accusations of abuse. Agents are instructed to behave in a businesslike manner, and that should be your approach as well.

What is businesslike?

Polite and confident, but sparing of speech. Do not make small talk, and do not volunteer any information. Don't talk about your family or your home. Respond only to the agent's direct questions, which should concern only the issues raised in the notification of examination. If the agent asks you questions on items that were not listed in the notification, you should request a second appointment rather than address them without preparation. (There is also a chance that this will prompt the agent to back off entirely on these additional questions.) Finally, you should also be aware that you have a kind of panic button available to you. At any time during the interview, you can state that you want to consult with a representative—accountant, attorney, whatever—and the agent must suspend the interview pending that consultation.

You want to give the impression of willingness to cooperate. You want to communicate your desire to help the agent do his job. Do this by answering any questions thoroughly and clearly, not by volunteering extra information. Do not feel that you must hurry through an answer. Take your time, and keep the notification letter, which enumerates the items under examination, before you. Remember, if the agent raises other questions, you should not feel pressured into answering them on the spot. "Because that item wasn't listed on the letter of notification, I'm not fully prepared to discuss it. I could discuss it at a second interview, which will allow me time to review the relevant records." If at any time you feel pressed for a response, back off and take whatever time is necessary to formulate an answer.

What I have said here is advice on verbal demeanor—a way of presenting yourself at the audit interview. It is not meant as a substitute for the professional counsel of an accountant or a lawyer. At the very least, you should consult a good tax guide publication—including those issued by the IRS itself—to become fully acquainted with your rights and responsibilities at an audit.

Words to Use

accept	*propose*
advice	*question*
amend	*rational*
answer	*reasonable*
backup	*reasoning*
calculate	*records*
clarify	*relate*
consult	*relevant*
cooperate	*report*
eager	*satisfy*
estimate	*standard*
explain	*submit*
file	*supply*
furnish	*support*
judgment	*usual*
justify	*willing*

Phrases to Use

acted on the advice I received	*nothing unusual in that*
be happy to	*review the supporting documents*
clear up	*standard practice*
eager to supply the necessary information	*supply what you require*
give you the answers	*take exception to*
good faith	*used my best judgment*
more specific	*whatever you need*
	you will find reasonable

Words to Avoid

afford	*guesstimate*
afraid	*lied*
bleed	*panic*
can't	*poor*
demand	*rip-off*
family	*robbery*
fudged	*terrified*
guess	*unreasonable*
guessed	*won't*

Phrases to Avoid

> *give me a break*
> *go easy on me*
> *have a heart*
> *let me tell you about myself*
> *made it up*
> *make an exception*

> *take a stab at*
> *tell you whatever you want*
>   *to hear*
> *try to understand my*
>   *position*
> *whatever you say*

Your Script

Agent: *As you know, the Service is questioning the deductions taken for home office space, personal computer purchases, and books. What do you have to say about these?*

You: *All are strictly used for business purposes. What, specifically, would you like me to show you by way of backup? I've brought a sheaf of photocopies.*

Agent: *Let's begin with receipts for books.*

You: *There are a lot of them. Those that specify titles, as you can see, are all related to my consulting business. I'd be happy to go through the titles with you.*

Agent: *Do you have any material to support your claim concerning the room in your house you use for an office?*

You: *I have Polaroids that show the setup. I think that constitutes reasonable backup.*

Agent: *I'd also like to know about deductions relating to a VCR.*

You: *I have backup material available. But since the VCR was not one of the items mentioned in the notification letter, I am not prepared to discuss it now. I need time to review my records relevant to that deduction and gather my backup material. I'd be happy to answer questions about the VCR at another interview.*

Responses to Anticipate

Because of the very specific and often technical nature of the audit process, it would be misleading to furnish a simple set of responses to anticipate and replies to them. You should be aware, however, that if you do not agree with the results of the audit examination you may request an immediate review by the examiner's supervisor. It is not obligatory that you and the IRS reach an agreement during the original examination. If you and the Service disagree, you will be sent a "thirty-day letter" explaining your right to appeal, a copy of the examination report, a waiver form, and IRS Publication 5, "Appeal Rights and Preparation of Protests for Unagreed Cases." Again, you may find it in your best interest at this point to consult a tax professional.

Your Landlord

The word *landlord*, a holdover from a darker age, is in itself intimidating, seeming to confer upon this individual feudal powers. And it is true that landlords run the gamut from paternal/maternal, to business-like, to negligent, to nasty. Yet it is well to remember that, beyond the emotional freight the landlord-tenant relation bears, it is at bottom a business deal, nothing more or less, and it obligates the landlord as much as it does you.

From the beginning of your relationship you want to communicate to the landlord that you are a financially responsible tenant who has the highest respect for his property. At the same time you need to convey that you are acutely concerned with the quality of your life, especially your home. You expect your landlord to recognize, appreciate, and respect this. Ideally, then, the landlord-tenant relationship is symbiotic—both parties benefit—and when things go smoothly, little communication is required. But, of course, glitches of varying magnitude will occur from time to time.

Let's begin with the circumstances that make it most necessary—but also most difficult—to communicate effectively with the landlord:

- You are going to be late with the rent.
- You've damaged some part of the landlord's property.
- Another tenant complains about you.

All three situations are embarrassing and make us want to avoid the landlord rather than seek contact with him. Yet speaking up on these occasions will do much to avert genuine catastrophe.

In one sense your landlord is no different from any of your other creditors. By contract, you owe him a certain sum each month. Yet the relationship is even more sensitive. Your falling behind on a loan payment, say, may inconvenience a creditor, but it does not prevent his continued collection of loans made to others, nor does it interfere with his making new loans.

Being late with the month's rent, however, may send a wave of angry panic through the landlord's heart. Not only is he out the money you owe him, but he is aware that you are occupying a property that is potentially profitable. He can't help thinking, If only I had rented to so-and-so. *She* wouldn't have stiffed me.

How do you head off this blend of anger and anxiety? Advise your landlord of any payment problem *before* the rent is due. Provide an explanation, apology, and, if possible, a proposal for partial payment with a promise to send the balance by a certain date. This does not guarantee to neutralize all bad feelings, but it will make the difference between mere annoyance and full-blown outrage.

Timely communication is also called for if you damage property. Explain the circumstances of the incident and the extent of the damage. Although you may be tempted to make the gesture of offering to pay for the damage (and, indeed, you may be obligated to do so), it is a better strategy to invite the landlord over to see the problem for himself. He may chalk it up to normal wear-and-tear and absorb the expense himself.

Even more embarrassing than dealing with damaged property is responding to a call from your landlord relaying a neighbor's complaint about you. Whether the complaint is justified or not, respond calmly and in two ways. First, ask for a full explanation of the complaint—all the particulars, including relevant dates. Second, express your wish that the neighbor had come to you first instead of pestering the landlord. Both responses suggest concern and that you are taking the complaint seriously. In addition, the second response tends to recruit the landlord into your camp rather than your neighbor's.

From this point, depending on circumstances, you need to go on to an explanation and an apology, including an assurance that the problem will not recur. Or, if the complaint is unjustified, you must relate "your side" of the story. How do you do this without sounding merely defensive? Stick to the facts instead of protesting your innocence or expressing your outrage. Don't call names, and don't call your neighbor a liar. Introduce the facts of the case by saying something like, "That's not true. What really happened . . . "

It is easy to understand having difficulty speaking to your landlord when you are (or believe that you are) in the wrong. But why do we often feel shy about asking for improvements, negotiating or renegotiating a lease, or even asking for necessary repairs? I can think of only two reasons. Landlords belong to that class of authority figures who, at some level of our consciousness, summon up the image of the parent. If we were reluctant to ask our parents for things, we will be similarly reluctant about asking our landlord. Second, strange as it may seem when we faithfully fork over a substantial rent check each month, many of us feel that we are living in the landlord's place, not in our own. This being the case, we feel—again, at some level of consciousness—that asking for improvements or more favorable lease terms is an imposition. In both cases, we are dealing with feelings.

Make no mistake, such feelings are quite real and cannot simply be dismissed. They can, however, be recognized and worked around.

It's hard to think of our home, the place we live, as part of a business arrangement. But for renters, that's just what it is, and, like any other such arrangement, it is subject to negotiation. It may help to begin on a positive note: "Mrs. Smith, I've really enjoyed living here, and I appreciate how responsive you are. I'd like to talk to you about negotiating a two-year lease this time." Even after you have surmounted the hurdle by making your request, landlords have a way of draining any follow-up energy through benign neglect. You may have to be persistent, using such phrases as, "Have you set a date for," "When can I expect," "Have you given more thought to," and so on.

Finally there is the special situation of the live-in landlord, the one who occupies an apartment in the building or, more usually, rents out part of his own house. Such a landlord may be more responsive to your requests, since he is in frequent contact with you. The usual problems that arise between landlords and tenants in this situation, however, concern issues of privacy. The landlord may find it difficult to relinquish completely that portion of the house you rent, and he may disapprove of the people you invite into "his" home. Indeed, it takes a very sensitive homeowning landlord to respect your privacy adequately. It is important to confront such issues. Again, begin as positively as possible, but don't beat around the bush. You also need to bring up specifics, rather than allude to vague feelings you may have.

Words to Use

apologize	negotiate
changes	pleasant
delay	pleasure
difficulty	problem
enjoy	regard
explain	renegotiate
inconvenienced	repair
inform	respect
investigate	responsive
issue	situation
necessary	timely
needed	

Phrases to Use

changes are necessary	expect my check by
enjoy living here	have a problem with

*it has been x years since x
was done
make the following
improvements
pleasure living here
renegotiate terms
repairs are needed as soon
as possible*

*report a problem with
speak with you
temporary difficulty
the problem is causing me
great inconvenience
this will not happen again
x is falling apart*

Words to Avoid

*can't
cheat
condemned*

*dishonest
liar
slum*

Phrases to Avoid

*can't pay
doesn't matter to me*

whatever you want to do

Your Script

1.

I am calling to tell you that I've had unexpected emergency medical expenses. This is going to mean that my December rent will be two weeks late. I'm very sorry. If it will help make the situation less inconvenient for you, I can pay $100 on the first—then the balance by the fifteenth. I would really be very grateful for your understanding in this matter.

Call in advance of a payment problem. Briefly explain the problem and its impact on your upcoming rent payment. Provide a date of payment and, if possible, make an offer of partial payment on time.

2.

You: *Mr. Flint, the apartment has not been painted since I moved in six years ago. It's looking pretty shabby, and I like to take pride in where I live.*

Landlord: *I don't think it's due for painting yet.*

You: *I'm willing to do the work myself, if you buy the paint.*

Facts are your most potent resource in negotiating with your landlord. Use them. Note the allusion to the tenant's character ("I like to take pride . . ."). If you meet resistance, be prepared to negotiate—but don't start off by making your best offer. This tenant expected to do the job himself, but instead of beginning that way, he used the offer as his fallback position.

Responses to Anticipate

I'm giving you a good deal. I'm not made of money.
Reply with:

☑ *I do enjoy living here, and because I do, I want to see that the place is well maintained. I'm not asking you to do anything that won't make a lasting improvement to your property.*

I don't care about what you have to say. I just want to stop hearing complaints from other tenants.
Reply with:

☑ *As I understand it, only Mrs. Carpenter has complained—one tenant out of eighteen in this building. Nevertheless, I can see where my guests might have made too much noise as far as she was concerned. I assure you, it won't happen again.*

In your lease, you promise to pay rent on time.
Reply with:

☑ *I'm aware of that, and, believe me, I don't like putting you in this position. But given the circumstances, I really have no choice. Just be assured that this is a one-time problem, and that I will be able to pay you by the eighteenth.*

Your Lawyer

No one, not even psychiatrists, charge more money for the privilege of conversation. Little wonder we are often frustrated by the sense that meetings with our legal counsel are less, far less, productive than they should be. It is beyond the scope of a general-purpose book like this to discuss the lawyer-client relationship when you are embroiled in criminal or high-stakes civil litigation. Of concern here are those occasions when you consult your lawyer on everyday questions: hammering out a contract or a lease, writing a will, seeking advice on the legality or advisability of an action or venture you are contemplating. Why are we so often nagged by questions about whether the trip to the lawyer was worth the expense?

The fact is that one has to wonder whether *any* legal information can be worth $200 and up per hour. There is little you can do about the rate your lawyer charges (beyond, of course, trying to negotiate something lower), but you can take steps to ensure that this literally precious time will be spent to best advantage.

Lawyers as a class are loathed as much as they are envied, and some are not averse to "churning" litigation—that is, generating work for themselves. But even these avaricious souls are not usually interested in profiting from patently unproductive hours of consultation. Generally speaking, your lawyer is not after a small but quick profit from you. She wants you for the long term; she wants to win one for the two of you, and she wants you to be satisfied.

The burden of achieving effective communication does not rest solely with you, but the process does begin with you. Faced with a thorny legal problem, we have a tendency to present ourselves to a lawyer as a patient might present himself to his doctor: passively.

Here I am and here it is. *You* figure us out.

Much time is wasted as your lawyer talks to you and sifts through your recent past. The bottom line is that you literally cannot afford to present yourself to your lawyer as a patient in search of a cure. You must begin the process. You must think through the issues you want to raise, then prepare as extensive and straightforward an outline as possible *prior to your visit*. Give your lawyer a copy of the outline as you run down the items for discussion.

Having ensured that each of the central issues will be raised, the next task is pinning down answers in a meaningful way. To whatever degree possible, coax your lawyer into quantifying her answers: "Seventy percent of the time, this happens"; "There are three possibilities"; "Of the two alternatives, the second one has the best chance of working out." The object is to get beneath the recommendations and glimpse the assumptions on which your lawyer is operating. This way your decisions will be better informed, based on the most detailed information available.

Perhaps it is disturbing to learn that you not only have to pay your lawyer a hefty sum for consultation, *you* also have to put in some hours preparing for the event yourself. All I can answer is that the benefits of preparation make the legal fees seem, if not a bargain, at least more reasonable. More importantly, by taking an active role in the discussion, you greatly increase your chances of obtaining the best possible results from your visit to your lawyer.

Words to Use

advice	*caution*
advise	*checklist*
aggressive	*evaluate*
alternatives	*explain*

issues
negotiate
options
outline
plan
precise
precisely
present

problem
proceed
quantify
safe
safety
satisfaction
strategy

Phrases to Use

best-case scenario
best guess
give me the percentages
how confident are you
issues to address
lay out for you
make a list

next move
pin down
pros and cons
what are the odds
what's the probability
worst-case scenario

Words to Avoid

basically
generally

shyster
tell

Phrases to Avoid

in general
let me talk to you
take all the time we need

tell me what I should do
what's my next move

Your Script

You: *Now that we've reviewed the outline, what are the potential consequences of their defaulting on the contract?*

Lawyer: *They wouldn't be pleasant.*

You: *Can you be more specific?*

Lawyer: *The worst-case scenario . . . they sue you for triple damages.*

You: *What do you see as the chances of that?*

Lawyer: *Slight chance.*

You: *Can you quantify that?*

Lawyer: *Maybe a 10-percent chance.*

Much of the success of a consultation with your lawyer depends on your own preparation. Even a good outline, however, cannot always guarantee that your lawyer will be easy to pin down to reasonably precise terms. Be persistent, working your lawyer as close to precision—which usually means quantification—as possible.

Responses to Anticipate

I can't be any more precise than this.
Respond with:

☑ *Are you sure? I want the highest-quality information you can give me.*

It's going to take me some time to formulate a plan.
Respond with:

☑ *What's your best guess of how long?*

That's something I cannot address.
Respond with:

☑ *What is your objection to speculating on it?*

The Loan Officer

You think you're uncomfortable when you apply for a loan? Try putting yourself in the loan officer's shoes.

You say you'd like that very much? Sitting there like some grand inquisitor? Or more like the bouncer for a *very* fancy nightclub, coolly deciding who will get in and who will not?

In reality, the loan officer is pulled in opposite directions by a difficult mission that makes inherently contradictory demands. She is expected, on the one hand, to loan money. That's how banks and other lending institutions stay in business. But she is also expected to keep the bank from making a bad or risky loan. In applying for a loan, you have an opportunity to make the tormented loan officer's job easier by doing your verbal best to enable her simply to say "yes."

Before we continue, let's dispense some necessary bad news. A good conversation with the loan officer does give you an edge, but the sad fact is that no amount of talk is likely to make up for a poor credit history or an income level that falls substantially below what the lending institution prescribes. That said, you should proceed in the expectation of getting the loan you want. Be aware that the lending institution will make its decision, for the most part, based on data that has very little to do with you as a person, but never *assume* that you will be rejected. True, your mother told you that if you have high hopes, you are sure to be disappointed. However, when you are seeking a loan, high hopes are better than none. Approach the loan officer not in a spirit of modest foot shuffling but with whatever air of confidence you can muster. Declare, "I will use the money to finance the start-up of . . ." Do not say, "If I get the loan, I will use the money . . ."

Since the days of the Greek tragedies, we have been cautioned against "hubris"—excessive self-confidence. It is good, we are told, to be modest and not to expect too much. The problem with modesty in the presence of a loan officer is that some of it might rub off on her. Contrary to what you may feel, she will not say to herself, "I'm going to shoot this arrogant clay pigeon down." She may, however, at some level of consciousness, perceive your modesty and bet-hedging as a lack of confidence: "If he has doubts about this loan, shouldn't I think twice?"

The first rule, then, is that good words are no substitute for good numbers. The second rule is that you should act as if good words will make all the difference.

Speak confidently, and dress as well as you possibly can. It is true that the wise American philosopher Henry David Thoreau cautioned us against undertaking "any enterprise that requires new clothes." But it is also true that Thoreau, in his wisdom, showed little interest in making money. In a money business, clothes are important. Looking poor will get you a few coins if you're out on the street, but in a banker's office, crazy as it may seem, it is the look of prosperity that attracts the money.

I don't mean to imply that you should rely wholly on style. What you say to the loan officer is largely determined by the questions she asks. Answer as positively as possible. The remarks you make should underscore highlights of your written loan application, or, if the conversation is in advance of the paperwork, your remarks should highlight key accomplishments related to this loan or your financial performance generally. The cardinal rule governing the content of your conversation with the loan officer is to show rather than tell. For the loan officer, words offer poor competition against numbers, but the words that perform best are the verbs and the nouns. Adjectives run a distant fourth place. To the loan officer they ring hollow and they smell of hype. You'll go further with, "In 1990, using seed money of $45,000, I put together a business that grosses $125,000 a year" than with "I am a determined, savvy, aggressive businessman."

Remember that your object is to help the loan officer do the part of her job that involves *making* loans. She needs no help with the part of her job that refuses loans. That she can do very well without your help, thank you. Accordingly, don't feel obliged to point out problems or to explain any financial glitches *she* fails to point out. When she does question you about these, do not gloss over them but, in as fact-based a manner as possible, put them in the best light you can find. "We did miss a payment on that credit card in 1985. My wife and I were traveling in Europe when the bill came. As you can see, the payment was less than sixty days late, and ever since then we have paid on time."

Finally, don't volunteer unsolicited information. As my salesman uncle used to say, "Once you've made the sale, shut up." You should, however, close the discussion by leaving it open: "If there is any other information you need, just call me."

Words to Use

balance
care
careful
compare
confident
context
cooperate
dependable
develop
explain
facilitate
facts
finance
growth
invest

market
numbers
partnership
performance
predictable
prudent
record
reliable
responsibility
safe
safety
stability
stable
study

Phrases to Use

examine the record
expedite the process
help you make the decision
high degree of reliability
invest the funds

look at past performance
make it possible for you to
make your job easier
predict the outcome
proven performance

Words to Avoid

allow
anxiety
anxious
assume
broke
desperate

doubt
eager
give
if
need
nervous

perhaps

risk

rush

scared

troubled

worry

Phrases to Avoid

assuming I get the money

assuming the loan goes
through

give me a chance

I desperately need cash

if I get the money

if it is possible

if, perhaps, you

if you can make the loan

I'm desperate

I really need these funds

let me have

take a chance

take the risk

Your Script

I believe my application speaks for itself, but I did want to point out a few highlights. My company currently has a client base of 545 stores, up from 467 last year. My gross is up by 18 percent over last year. And my business is stable. We've been in operation eight years now. We're at the point where it is not only desirable but prudent to expand. I'd like the opportunity to work with you to finance our growth.

Emphasize facts rather than self-generated value judgments—which means that you should be free with strong nouns and verbs but sparing with adjectives. To whatever degree you can manage, draw a picture of the lending institution as your partner—not your skinflint would-be sugar daddy.

Responses to Anticipate

You will need to explain some late payments that show up on your credit report.

Reply with:

☑ *My current credit situation is clean, of course, and has been for some time. Let me review the report, and I will be happy to write a letter explaining any glitches.*

I don't think that it will be possible to accommodate you at this time.

Reply with:

☑ *What can I do or supply that will make it possible?*

Let me ask you pointblank. Why should we make this loan?
Reply with:

☑ *It's the very definition of a good business decision: a good investment for you, and an important opportunity for me.*

Your Neighbor

I grew up on the West Side of Chicago in the early 1960s. We lived in a modest row-house development, and I remember that, on summer evenings, the neighbors would sit on their stoops and talk to one another. It was "small talk" of the best kind: politics, the city, neighborhood goings on, business, cars, and so on. I remember our community of neighbors as a tight-knit, genial group. It was easy to ask for a favor, tensions were negligible, and serious arguments were few.

I don't think such neighborhoods are as common nowadays. We live in a time and in places that discourage the development of a genuine community of neighbors. For most of us, the result is a vague sense of discomfort about the people who live only a few hundred feet (or less) from us. For many others, however, the result is a more extreme breakdown of communication: a dispute.

How do you speak up to a neighbor? The first thing to remember is that the neighbor-neighbor relationship is long term, even if you rarely talk to one another. Quite possibly, you will be near your neighbor for a very long time indeed. In contrast, the issues involved in any dispute are probably quite short term. Therefore, when some matter of concern or even a full-blown dispute arises, the object must be to address the issues rather than the person.

Before you even approach your neighbor, you should attempt to find within the issues—or even within the dispute—some areas of common interest and benefit. For example, your neighbor is frequently away from his house for days at a stretch, but he fails to stop his newspaper and mail delivery. You are concerned that the accumulation of papers and mail will attract burglars. Why should you be concerned? It's *his* house, after all. True, but it is also a fact that once burglars hit a particular house in the neighborhood, they have a nasty habit of working the whole block. Your neighbor's papers may eventually get *you* robbed.

Now, if you seriously start thinking this way, you'll soon find yourself getting quite angry. Your neighbor will start to seem irresponsible, thoughtless—a local hazard. This is precisely how matters of concern grow into disputes, increasingly bitter disputes no longer based on the underlying issues but strictly on personalities.

Instead of taking this approach, you could talk to your neighbor and point out your concern over the security of *his* house and, incidentally, of the neighborhood. Then suggest that he stop his mail and papers when he goes away. Such a conversation may or may not produce results. But there is an even better way. Visit your neighbor, tell him your concerns, then point out that you realize what a royal pain it is to go to the post office and stop your mail and to call the newspaper and suspend delivery. This being the case, offer to collect the newspapers and mail for him. Yes, this does involve some work on your part—though very little, actually—but what it creates is a commonality of interest that transforms a potential dispute into an occasion of genuine neighborliness. You get what you want; you also help your neighbor; and, in the process, you create a partnership.

With imagination, even more serious disputes can be approached this way. But why wait until one arises? Find some common causes—a problem with weeds, a dirty hallway, whatever—and attack it together.

Words to Use

aid	investigate
alert	lend
allow	mutual
answer	offer
assist	permit
benefit	prefer
borrow	problem
collaborate	rather
consider	solution
cooperate	suggest
explore	suggestion
help	together

Phrases to Use

do this together	investigate the alternatives
explore the options	make our lives easier
for a common benefit	makes me uncomfortable
get together	rather not
give some thought to	the two of us
improve conditions	work together
in common	

Words to Avoid

complain *selfish*
complaint *uncooperative*
irresponsible

Phrases to Avoid

if you don't, I'll . . . *you'd better not*
I have a complaint *you have no choice*
major problem *you have no right*
my rights *you have to*
you can't *you must not*
you'd better

Your Script

1.

You: *I love your dog, but I don't like what he's been leaving in my backyard. I'm also concerned because I see him running across the street. It's only a matter of time before somebody hits him.*

Neighbor: *I'm sorry about your yard. You know, I like him to have his freedom. I'll be happy to help you clean up.*

You: *I appreciate that very much. But you're going to be over here more often than you want to be, I suspect. We really should do something about the situation. Have you considered any of the alternatives to just letting him run free? I've seen those extra-long leashes that reel in and out. They don't get tangled, and they should give your dog enough rope to have the full freedom of your yard.*

Never attack your neighbor's pet verbally or otherwise. Establish a commonality of interest by announcing your affection for the animal, but be clear in explaining what you will and will not tolerate. Collaborate in the resolution of the problem by offering helpful suggestions.

2.

I hate to be the one to make this phone call, but I figured I'd better do it before someone else in the neighborhood does. Your party sounds like a lot of fun, but it is getting pretty loud. I don't want to step on anybody's good time, but could you hold it down?

No one likes a killjoy—but, then, no one likes noisy neighbors, either. Here is a way to make a request for peace seem like you're doing your neighbor a favor.

Responses to Anticipate

I have a right to do what I want. I live here, too.
Reply with:

☑ *What is your objection to living more cooperatively?*

There's nothing I can do about it.
Reply with:

☑ *Perhaps, but before we give up, I suggest we brainstorm some alternatives together.*

Can I borrow your snow blower?
Reply with:

☑ *Of course. Please put it back in the garage when you've finished with it. It takes regular gas.*

Can I borrow your snow blower?
Reply with:

☑ *I'll be happy to lend it to you just as soon as I've finished with it. That won't be until later this afternoon.*

Can I borrow your snow blower?
Reply with:

☑ *This thing has been in and out of the repair shop over and over again. I'm sorry, but I really am uncomfortable lending it. It's costing me a fortune.*

The Police Officer

It is tempting to generalize about cops, and everybody does it. The cop is the blue knight. The cop is a storm trooper in a blue suit. And everything in between.

The only safe generalization to make is that a cop is a human being doing a job that subjects him to varied and intense physical as well as emotional pressures. A cop is also accustomed to being met with—at the very best—dislike and even fear.

This book is not the place to turn in order to find out what to say to a cop who puts you under arrest for robbing a bank. Seek the answer to that one from a good criminal attorney. Nor is it my intention to tell you how to talk your way out of a traffic ticket. But following the communication pointers given here may help keep you from talking yourself *into* one.

If you ask a woman how she feels when a policeman stops her, she will generally admit that she feels stress, even fear. A man, on the other hand, will tend to tell you that he feels anger. Does this mean that men are stronger than women? No. It means that, in this case at least, woman are more honest than men when it comes to relating feelings. The fact is that most of us feel a rush of anxiety when we see the flashing lights in the rearview mirror. The experience may be accompanied by anger—and even a headstrong impulse to defy authority—but, at bottom, even if we are quite innocent of wrongdoing, we feel fear.

In most jurisdictions in the United States, and under most conditions, this is, of course, an overreaction. Generally, a police officer making a traffic stop is trained to be polite and businesslike. His job is to issue the summons efficiently, without a lecture, and without subjecting you to undue delay. If anyone in this transaction has reason to be fearful, it is the police officer. We have all read newspaper stories about officers getting blown away when they pull a car over. Recently I asked a detective friend of mine to tell me what he thought was the most dangerous thing a police officer does.

"Car stops," he answered.

Be aware, then, when you are pulled over and your heart is pounding, that the police officer, somewhere inside himself, is also feeling the stress of potential danger.

That is not the only source of his anxiety. Even if you're not packing a gun, the officer knows that you're not pleased to see him. Can you imagine being in a business in which each of your customers is at worst a potential killer and at best *very* unhappy? Ninety-nine percent of police officers will exhibit no outward signs of this internal tumult. That's part of being a professional. But the stresses are present, and you should be aware of them.

Before we continue you might ask if there is any point to all this. That is, can you do anything to change the officer's mind about giving you a ticket? The answer is an unqualified "probably not."

Traffic violations abound; police officers don't generally have to invent them. More importantly, it is a police officer's job to spot violations and issues summonses accordingly. But it is not his job ultimately to judge guilt or innocence. Accepting the ticket is never an admission of guilt. If you honestly believe yourself innocent, accept the ticket, respond to it at the appropriate time with a "not guilty" plea, and avail yourself of the opportunity of your day in court. Don't argue the case with the police officer.

Having said all this, it is a fact that the police officer can often choose among a range of offenses—some less serious than others—with which he can charge you. Let me offer a personal example.

I was driving on a suburban street. I was in the left lane approaching an intersection, and I decided that I needed to turn right. I signaled—very briefly—and started to enter the right lane, but caught a glimpse of a car in that lane. I swerved back into the left lane, changed signals, and made a left turn instead of a right.

Bad driving? Maybe. Sloppy driving? Definitely. In any case, that's when I saw the flashing lights. I pulled over.

The first thing I did was perfectly correct. I did not get out of the car. Police officers prefer that you wait for them in your vehicle. There are three reasons for this. First, your getting out is a sign not of cooperation but of potential aggression. Second, the officer has several things to do before he can attend to the business of actually issuing the summons. He must call in your license plate number to check for outstanding warrants, violations, and so on. He needs to have this information *before* he approaches you. He does not want you hovering near his window while he is waiting to find out whether or not you are wanted for murder in any of the fifty states. Third, and most important, you are safest in your car. It is dangerous to stand by the side of the road—especially along a busy highway. During the transaction, the officer is properly concerned for his own safety; it will not help your case to add to his anxiety concern over your safety as well.

So I did that much right. I stayed in the car. What I did next, however, was unnecessarily provocative. The cop approached; I felt anxiety and irritation. What I said was, in and of itself, harmless enough: "What's the problem, officer?"

The *problem*, it turned out, was my tone of voice. It was angry, combative, and irritable. And, in context, the question was simply stupid: I had swerved into another lane, having signaled late, then I swerved back into the other lane. I don't believe I came close to causing an accident, but to anyone outside my vehicle, my driving would have appeared questionable.

Things got worse. The officer asked for my license, registration, and insurance ID. All was in order, except for my insurance ID—the latest one was at home in an unopened envelope. The one I had in my glove compartment had expired.

The officer went back to his car briefly and returned with a summons for $30. He handed it to me with the following remark:

"A lot depends on attitude. I pulled you over because of what you did at the corner. I wanted to see if anything was wrong. You jumped down my throat. Because you don't have a current insurance ID, I could have the car impounded. That's up to my judgment. As it is, I'll just give you this summons."

My "attitude" was made manifest in the space of four words. They weren't even particularly unpleasant words. But what I didn't realize was the power of the emotion behind them.

You won't realize it either, when something like this happens to you. In such an inevitably charged atmosphere, it is best to keep relatively silent, responding politely to questions only and volunteering little or nothing on your own. Do not admit guilt, and unless you think you really are the victim of a misunderstanding or misinterpretation, don't protest your innocence. Remain patiently in your car, and it's not a bad idea to keep your hands conspicuously visible.

If you do feel that you were stopped without good reason, go ahead and tell the officer. "May I explain what happened?" is a good non-threatening way to begin. In general, perhaps even more than most any other professional, police officers respond positively to courtesy—even if it's only polite silence.

Not all contact with police personnel comes in such unpleasant situations. If you live in a community where you regularly see the cop on the beat, give him or her a friendly hello. It won't get you any special favors, but it will get beyond the uniform to the person, and that is never a bad thing.

Words to Use

ask	*inadvertent*
assist	*no*
aware	*problem*
certainly	*talk*
cooperate	*tell*
error	*unaware*
explain	*yes*
help	

Phrases to Use

good afternoon	*Is there a problem?*
good evening	*I think you should know*
good morning	*about*

let me tell you about　　　*What can I do?*
may I explain　　　　　　*What do you need?*

Words to Avoid

accident　　　　　　　*ridiculous*
accidental　　　　　　*stupid*
afford　　　　　　　　*thoughtless*
arrest　　　　　　　　*trouble*
fault　　　　　　　　　*unfair*
guilty　　　　　　　　*wrong*
mistake

Phrases to Avoid

Are you blind?　　　　　　　*there will be big trouble*
Can't you overlook this?　　　　　*over this*
I can't afford another ticket.　　*this is ridiculous*
I didn't do anything.　　　　　　*you're out of line*
It's my fault.　　　　　　　　　*you're wrong*
It was an accident.　　　　　　　*your word against mine*
I wasn't thinking.　　　　　　　*you've got the wrong person*
no justice

Your Script

You: *Good morning, officer.*
Officer: *Would you please show me your license and registration?*
You: *Of course.*
Officer: *Are you aware that you made an illegal right turn?*
You: *No, I am not aware of it.*
Officer: *It's marked.*
You: *I didn't see the sign.*
Officer: *It's relatively new.*
You: *I wonder if that fact is worth bringing up with the judge. It should be marked more clearly.*
Officer: *What you bring up with the judge is up to you.*

This conversation did not avoid a ticket, though it represents about as far as you can reasonably go to avoid getting one when you are, indeed, guilty. If there are extenuating circumstances, bring them up. But you should not use such circumstances in an overt attempt to talk your way out of a ticket. The officer is more likely to dismiss your explanation as just another lame excuse. The best you can hope for is that your remarks will prompt the officer to reconsider issuing the

AND EVERYONE ELSE • 167

summons, and the least you can expect is that a polite reply will minimize the citation insofar as this is within the police officer's discretion.

Responses to Anticipate

I'm just doing my job.
Reply with:

☑ *I understand. I just thought you'd want to hear my side before you
write me up.*

I had you clocked at seventy-four miles per hour.
Reply with:

☑ *I understand, but I don't think I was going that fast.*

*I could write you up for the damaged taillight, but I'm just going to
ask you to go—now—to a garage and get that fixed. No summons—
this time.*
Reply with:

☑ *I appreciate that very much, officer.*

The Waiter or Waitress

At least two things can go wrong with the waiter-patron relationship.
You may find yourself served by a rude waiter, or you may find the
service slow and inept. If you are having a particularly bad experience, you may be subjected to a combination of the two.

Begin your transaction with the waiter or waitress politely and
efficiently. "I'd like the trout, please" is much better than "Let me
have the trout" or "Bring me the trout." Unless you are acquainted
with the waiter (perhaps you are a "regular" at the restaurant), don't
detain him with unnecessary conversation. You may think of such
small talk as a nice gesture, but the one thing a waiter or waitress
doesn't have is time to waste. Don't detain him or her. It is also important to avoid such patronizing words as "dear," "honey," "sweet-
heart," and the like, as well as such overly coy phrases like "would
you be so kind" or "if it wouldn't be too much trouble." Many waiters
and waitresses resent being patronized even more than they dislike
out-and-out abuse from customers.

Polite, professional communication with a waiter or waitress
does not, of course, guarantee satisfactory service. When the worst
happens, what do you say to a rude waiter?

The temptations are endless, but remember, your goal is not to avenge a personal affront but simply to get your meal in a timely and accurate fashion. Rudeness is meant to elicit one of two responses: to intimidate you or to provoke hostility from you. You can simply refuse to take this gambit by ignoring the rudeness altogether. If this works for you, fine; but for many, ignoring bad service detracts from the pleasure of an evening out. There is another alternative. Don't fold and don't flare, but respond with something entirely unexpected: "What is your objection to serving us politely?"

The last thing a rude person wants or expects is that his rudeness will be met with rationality—will become, in effect, the subject of analytical discussion. Such a response may well defuse the situation and even elicit an apology on the spot.

Slow service is often not the fault of the waiter or waitress, and you should never begin by attacking him or her for it. If you feel that you have been waiting too long for your meal, call the waiter over, using eye contact and an upraised finger (don't snap your fingers or flag him down with a wave). A good line at this point is, "Is there a problem in the kitchen?" This question lets the waiter know that you are losing patience, but that you aren't losing patience with *him*. It unites the two of you against a third party—"the kitchen"—and, therefore, comes across more as a request for assistance than a criticism.

If this initial approach fails, summon the waiter again. Resort to the facts this time: "It has been twenty-five minutes since you took our order. This isn't an acceptable level of service."

After another ten minutes, call the waiter again and ask him to send you the maitre d', captain, or manager. Again, take a factual approach with him, explaining how long you've been waiting and that you find such service unacceptable. Make it *his* problem.

One final waiter-patron issue may at first seem to have less to do with the waiter or waitress than with the chef or cook. Some diners actually relish sending back an unsatisfactory meal—whether they want it cooked differently or are rejecting it outright. Most of us, however, feel uncomfortable doing this. Yet the truth is that you should expect to enjoy your meal. If it is not satisfactory, you have every right to reject it.

Now, while an unacceptable meal is not your waiter's fault —unless he took down the wrong order information—you do have to work through the waiter to send the meal back. Be careful to assign responsibility properly. "Waiter, please ask the chef to make this well done, as I requested."

Words to Use

acceptable

adequate

delay

difficulty

excellent

please

problem

recommend

service

thank you

unacceptable

unsatisfactory

Phrases to Use

expedite service

not happy with

not satisfied with

not satisfied with the quality

pressed for time

problem with

unacceptable service

we have been waiting for
___ minutes

without delay

Words to Avoid

awful

bad

fault

incompetent

obnoxious

outraged

outrageous

rude

terrible

Phrases to Avoid

Can we get some service
here?

don't want to be a bother,
but

get moving

hate to bother you

I'm not accustomed to be
treated so rudely

not paying for

put a move on it

take your time

unheard of

when you get a chance

Your Script

1.

You: *Waiter, we placed our order twenty minutes ago. What's the problem in the kitchen?*

Waiter: *I don't know. We're very busy.*

You: *I can see that. But twenty minutes is a long time to wait for lunch. We're all due back at the office. Can you please check on it?*

2.

Waiter: *Haven't you made up your minds yet?*

You: *What is your objection to doing your job politely and pleasantly?*

3.

You: *Please take this back to the kitchen and point out to the chef that the shrimp are underdone.*

Waiter: *I'm sorry.*

You: *It's not your fault. But please ask him to put them on a few minutes more. Thanks.*

Responses to Anticipate

I'm sorry. I'm new here.

Reply with:

☑ *You're doing fine—if you can just do what you can to expedite the service a bit. We've been waiting twenty minutes.*

This is not my table.

Reply with:

☑ *Wait just a minute, please. Would you ask our waiter to come over, then?*

I've only got two hands.

Reply with:

☑ *I can see that you're busy. I'm just asking you not to forget us here. We've also got things to do.*

The Wine Snob

He—and it *is* almost always a he—is the quintessential snob. Wine is one of those areas of interest that blend bona fide hard knowledge with a bully's ability to persuade, intimidate, and "snow." The wine snob pretends to mastery of arcane facts and exquisite taste. His object may be relatively harmless: to impress you and everyone else. Or it may be more sinister, annoying, and obnoxious: to show you up and put you down.

It is a wonderful thing to have friends with expertise in some of the finer things of life—love of good food, or inside information about where to get the best clothes at the lowest prices, what shows to see, and what wines to enjoy. A connoisseur crosses the line into snobbery, however, when he uses his knowledge—or his assumed knowledge— to intimidate. This is not acceptable behavior, and you should not have to tolerate it.

How do you combat a wine snob? You could learn something

about wines, of course, and fight fire with fire. Or you could simply invade his world by challenging him with intellectual demands. For the beauty of dealing with any snob, but especially a wine snob, is that you need no real knowledge yourself to call his bluff. Don't make up information, but ask questions and challenge answers *as if* you speak from knowledge. You'll find that doing so can turn an evening of intimidation into a mild, but nevertheless exhilarating, triumph over tyranny.

Words to Use

bland	*opinion*
bouquet	*palate*
disagree	*partly*
dry	*perhaps*
experience	*pleasant*
fruity	*possibly*
full-bodied	*Really?*
innocuous	*robust*
lackluster	*sometimes*
lifeless	*taste*
nose	

Phrases to Use

Are you sure?	*I don't think so*
clearly inferior	*not convinced*
clearly superior	*not to my knowledge*
don't you think	*not to my taste*
for you, perhaps	*on the dry side*
grown tired of it	*rather bland*
have never been convinced	*seems to me inferior*
I can't believe that	

Words to Avoid

best	*loathe*
despise	*love*
hate	*snob*
huh?	*worst*

Phrases to Avoid

defer to your knowledge	*I don't know much, but I*
don't know	*know what I like*
don't know much about	*I guess I'm just not*
wines	*knowledgeable*

*I'll take your word for it   you know best
my favorite*

Your Script

Snob: *You're not actually going to serve that stuff, are you?*
You: *I certainly am.*
Snob: *It's thin—not at all a good year.*
You: *I don't agree. I find it rather full-bodied, though dry.*

Reply with neutral but appropriate terminology. Why not try simply contradicting what the snob says? Stand his pronouncements on their heads.

Responses to Anticipate

Where did you learn about wine?
Reply with:

☑ *By drinking it and thinking about what I like and don't like—
learning to trust my taste.*

I wouldn't have this in my cellar.
Reply with:

☑ *Really? I find it quite refreshing without being overwhelming.*

Index